Heart
Soul Mind
Strength

Heart
Soul Mind
Strength

50 CREATIVE WORSHIP IDEAS FOR YOUTH GROUPS

Jenny Baker

MONARCH
BOOKS

Oxford, UK & Grand Rapids, Michigan, USA

First published in the UK in 2008 by Monarch Books
(a publishing imprint of Lion Hudson plc),
Wilkinson House, Jordan Hill Road, Oxford OX2 8DR.
Tel: +44 (0)1865 302750 Fax: +44 (0)1865 302757
Email: monarch@lionhudson.com
www.lionhudson.com

ISBN: 978–1-85424–899-2 (UK)
ISBN: 978–0-8254–6302-0 (USA)

Distributed by:
UK: Marston Book Services Ltd, PO Box 269, Abingdon, Oxon OX14 4YN;
USA: Kregel Publications, PO Box 2607, Grand Rapids, Michigan 49501

Unless otherwise stated, Scripture quotations are taken from the Holy Bible,
Today's New International Version, © 2001, 2005 by the International Bible Soci-
ety. Used by permission of Hodder & Stoughton Ltd. All rights reserved.

This book has been printed on paper and board independently
certified as having come from sustainable forests.

The views expressed by the author do not necessarily represent the views of the
partner organisations.

British Library Cataloguing Data
A catalogue record for this book is available from the British Library.

Printed and bound in Malta by Gutenberg Press.

For Lydia,
who has taught me so much about the love and presence of God

Contents

Acknowledgements

With thanks and respect to everyone who has been part of Grace over the years, for creating a space for worship, creativity, participation, challenge and growth in Christ. Many of these ideas have been developed within the Grace community or have been inspired through my involvement in it, and I have acknowledged individuals where appropriate in the footnotes. Thanks too to Martin Saunders, a series editor who actually got involved in the creation of this book. And love and admiration to the men in my life, Jonny, Joel and Harry, who never fail to amaze me with their creativity, determination and passion for life in all its fullness.

FOREWORD

Martin Saunders

Christian youth work involves a *lot* of different things. Relationship building, fun, taxi-driving, administrating, refereeing, listening, trip-organising, eating, game-inventing, planning, counselling, talking, explaining breakages to the PCC... the list goes on. Youth workers must be multi-disciplined multi-taskers who thrive on a ministry that most sane people would steer well clear of. At the heart of what we do as youth workers though is one essential job that has literally been entrusted to us by God – the role of developing young faith.

Having been involved in Christian youth work for a number of years now, I've got a pretty good handle on bad faith development. Through bitter experience, I've got a lengthening list of the stuff that *doesn't* work.

Faith isn't developed through attending a lot of meetings. Faith isn't developed by watching a charismatic youth pastor 'doing their thing' at the front of a venue. Faith isn't developed by wearing Christian t-shirts, listening to Christian music, and eating Biblically-referenced foodstuffs. Those aren't the building blocks of a faith that will endure from childhood to deathbed, yet if we're honest, most of us have been guilty of those kinds of substitutions in youth work at one time or another.

The vision behind this book is to help you, with plenty of your own hard work and some divine inspiration, to get involved with some genuine faith development. And as far as I understand it – from what the Bible tells me and from experience – the only thing that can develop a young person's faith is spending time with God. That's what this book is about – finding creative ways to bring young people into his presence. Not in a weird, abstract way, but – as is Jenny Baker's gift – in a way that reminds us that it's actually the most normal thing in the world.

Jenny is a youth worker and a creative who doesn't go in for big names, nominal spirituality or the Christian Brand. The integrity she brings to these ideas therefore infuses them with a real usefulness – they connect with ordinary young people, and then connect them to their heavenly father.

If we want young people to develop a faith that lasts, we need to get them into the habit and the mind of spending time with God. These tried and tested creative ideas will help you to do that.

Don't be afraid that many of these ideas involve concepts like silence, reflection, contemplation. Of course young people enjoy noise, mess and chaos, but they also thrive when we trust them to explore more reflective spirituality. A life full of noise, mess and chaos still needs moments of pause – this book gives you some tools to discover the unexpected joy of quiet young people!

The other thing this book provides is a set of resources for you to work through together with your volunteer team. What Jenny is wisely suggesting here is that it's not just young people who need to spend more time with God; as the people who are seeking to model a different way, we too must be growing closer to him. I encourage you to adapt and use this second set of resources with volunteer youth workers; cell leaders, and anyone else who looks like they might need a little spiritual invigoration.

Our deep longing as youth workers is to see the young people who 'graduate' from our youth ministries, keeping on in the faith long after they've left us. I believe that through developing a deep, reflective and Christ-centred faith with them, and through helping them into habits of prayer, worship, Bible-reading and silence, that's exactly what we'll see.

Introduction

Worship

Worship is the whole of our lives, lived for God. It's not confined to church buildings or Sundays, or even candle-encrusted emerging evenings in the back rooms of pubs. We can worship through our work, our relationships, our campaigning, our spending, our digging the allotment. However, this book is unashamedly concerned with the times when people gather to worship God and covers just one aspect of worship.

Worship is where we experience the reality of who God is and the reality of who we are; where we offer God every part of our complicated lives as best we can; where we align all that we are and all that we have with all that God calls us to. It's where we express our love and adoration of God, and where we are reminded of and receive God's love. Worship requires honesty and vulnerability from us and from God. It's a place of connection between our deepest selves and God's Spirit. Sometimes worship can be a challenging and uncomfortable place; at other times it can feel as if we have finally come home. Sometimes we'll be overwhelmed with the love and presence of God; at other times worship will seem bleak and cold.

Often we think of worship as what we do. It is singing in a particular style that we're used to. It has a structure that we're familiar with. It's led by people that we know and respect. It has a flavour that we've grown accustomed to.

In the last decade, however, people have been experimenting with creative expressions of worship that have questioned those assumptions. This exploration has not been simply about exchanging one style of worship for another. It has been asking more elemental questions about the structure and substance of worship and who creates it; about who participates in worship and what they discover there. These are some of the insights that I think we have learned.

Creating Worship is Part of our Worship
Spending time with others exploring themes from the Bible that we want to focus on in a service, and creating spaces and materials that enable others to encounter God, are not divorced from what happens when people gather to worship. Creative worship may be more time-consuming and even more costly, but the resources invested in it are a valuable gift offered to God in worship and to the community you serve.

Authentic Worship Arises from the Life of a Community

There are some people who frown on books like these, because of the risk that people will simply try to reproduce what has worked for others. I think there needs to be a generosity that shares ideas as a way of broadening horizons and as a spark for other people's imaginations. But you will need to discover for yourself the flavour of worship that is authentic to who you collectively are as a part of the body of Christ. You may begin with some of these ideas, but you will adapt them, subvert them, improve them and surpass them, as you explore together what it means to worship God in your location among the people whom God has called together. You need to be aware of your own context and culture and of the specific gifts that people in your community have, which will be different from those of the place where many of these ideas were formed. You need to start with what you've got and develop from there, blending new ideas with what is familiar, in order to take people along with you.

We Need to Reimagine the Role of Worship Leader

Leading worship becomes the task of creating rich spaces where God is revealed, providing the stimuli of words, images, music and objects that point people towards God, but that give them the space to discover God for themselves and give God space to engage with us. Leading worship is about relinquishing control and letting God in, in ways that we may not have expected. It's risky. It's about engaging fully with worship ourselves, in humility, in the middle of what is happening, not about being exposed and separate on a platform at the front.

There is a Mystery to Worship We Cannot Control

We don't know what people will bring to gathered worship and we can't control what they discover or experience there. Worship will be a multi-layered experience without fixed outcomes, where people encounter God in different ways according to their needs and the level of their willingness to engage. Of course we will plan to focus on specific themes, or explore particular Bible passages, as leaders of services have always done. Beyond that, we have to stand back and allow God to be God.

We Need to Create Spaces for Participation

There can be something very passive about singing songs that others have chosen, echoing words that someone else has written, to music that someone else is playing. Creative worship constructs environments that invite an active participation from those who are there, while also allowing people to disengage, if that's what they want. It calls for a response – which can be uncomfortable for some people, who would prefer to remain undisturbed and anonymous. But it's that active participation that empowers people to move on in their walk with God, without needing an expert to tell them what to do or how to do it.

Everyone Can Join In

Talking about our life story and our relationship with God as a journey is a very familiar metaphor, but it's a good one. All of us are moving towards or away from God, and at some point on that journey some of us will become followers of Jesus who receive the gift of eternal life that God offers us. Wherever we are on that journey, we can engage in worship: opening ourselves up to who God is and responding to what we discover about God. People who would not identify themselves as Christians can participate in this type of creative worship and they will be drawn into the sweet presence of God as they do.

The Structure of This Book

This book is organized into five different chapters, each of which contains ten ideas. There are ideas for moments of intentional prayer; ideas for worship services; ideas for creatively reading and exploring the Bible with young people; ideas for contemplative exercises that encourage young people to be still in God's presence; and then there are ideas for use with your youth team, to help build relationships and unlock creativity.

Each idea begins with a one-line description, a list of materials and some thoughts to explain the context, or where the idea came from.

Then comes an indication of the amount of effort involved in each idea. Clearly you need to read through each idea in advance of using it and decide whether it needs any adaptation for your group. Bear in mind what I've said above: that the most authentic worship will be what comes out of the creative crucible of your community. Having said all that, this is what to expect for the effort involved:

- ● ● ● Little preparation or materials needed: for many of these ideas, all you need is this book.
- ● ● ● Needs some advance preparation and some clearing up afterwards. You will need to tell people about some ideas in advance of the session where you use them, so that they can bring something or arrive prepared.
- ● ● ● Needs a fair amount of work and preparation, but it will be worth it!

After the instructions on how to carry out the idea come some links to Bible passages that help to connect it to God's word. Then there's a 'Hand it Over' section, which expands on how you can get young people involved in the execution of the idea, or on developing it further after the session.

I haven't told you how long each idea will take, because that depends so much on your group and the way in which you develop it. I'm sure you can work that out for yourselves.

What This Book Doesn't Give You

I deliberately haven't suggested specific music tracks that you can play alongside these ideas – for three reasons. Firstly, music is such a personal choice. You need to find tracks that you and your group like and respond to. Secondly, although you can't beat the classics, any suggestions I could make would quickly become dated. And thirdly, sourcing music for worship really isn't my thing. There are people at Grace who are far more gifted at that than I am, and for whom music is their passion. There will be people like that in your community; get them involved in finding music to complement the spaces for worship and prayer that you create. But do encourage them to look beyond the Christian community for good music. When young people hear music from their own world in worship, it helps them to feel at home and also reframes that music for them. The next time they hear it on their ipod or the radio, they'll be reminded of the worship and the connection they found with God.

You'll also need to find people who can create visuals to enhance your worship – projections, animations, photos and film loops. Many young people have access to multimedia equipment at school, and increasingly at home, and can rustle up a slideshow in the time it takes you to set up the data projector.

CHAPTER 1

Prayer

Prayer and worship are so interwoven that it can be difficult to separate them out. These activities create space for moments of intentional prayer; times when we address God directly with our concerns and requests in response to the invitation that God gives us. We come to God in confidence, knowing that we are loved and accepted, and knowing that God hears us and will respond, even though that may be in ways we don't expect.

Sometimes corporate prayer involves one person praying on behalf of those gathered, or a few people contributing spoken prayers while most people pray silently. Most of the ideas described here provide opportunities for everyone to participate more actively at different levels, depending on where they are in relationship with God. Many of them also symbolize what is happening in the prayer, helping to make more concrete and tangible an interaction that is in essence invisible and mysterious. They help people participate in prayer more holistically: with their bodies, their actions and their creativity as well as their words.

Tied in Knots

What Happens?

People tie a knot in a string for each worry on their mind. They then swap this with a partner, who prays for them as they untie the knots.

Effort Involved

Materials Needed

- A piece of string or rope about 1 metre long for each person.
- You may like to play some instrumental music in the background during this activity.

Some Thoughts

Worry is such a waste of time. It doesn't change anything or achieve anything, but it's so difficult not to do it! Often we go over our concerns in our minds again and again, exploring all the 'What ifs?', imagining the worst-case scenarios, getting tense and focusing inward. But Jesus said, 'Do not worry,' and Paul said, 'Do not be anxious.' God knows our needs and will take care of them. We need to let go of our worries and learn to trust God.

You're not suggesting through this activity that worries are easily solved, or that once each person has been prayed for then all their problems will magically disappear. What you are inviting them to do is to let go of their worries: to hand them over and to pray for someone else's concerns, taking their focus off themselves and onto someone else.

You may feel it's appropriate to get people to talk briefly about what is represented in their knotted strings and to name their concerns to each other. Decide whether that will work for your group.

Thick string or rope will create large knots and a striking visual representation of how tangled our thinking can become.

How to Do it

Explain what this activity is about: that it's an invitation to bring to God all the things that are worrying us or causing us concern. Invite people to collect a piece of string or rope and find a space.

Invite people to tie a knot in their pieces of string for each worry as they pray about it, telling God about their concern and that they want to trust God. Remind them not to tie the knots too tight. Allow people six or seven minutes to identify their worries and tie the knots.

Then tell people to swap strings with someone else, handing over their worries and letting go of them. (If you have an odd number of people in your group, then get a three to share their strings among them.) Now each person undoes the knots in the string just received. As they do so they pray, thanking God that God cares for the person who tied these knots and will answer their prayers. They could pray too that the person whose string they are unravelling will be able to receive God's peace. It's often easier to have faith that God will deal with someone else's problems than with your own; as they pray they should also acknowledge that God will do for them what they are praying God will do for their friend.

Then each person gives the straight piece of string back to its original owner, saying some words of blessing as they do so. They could use words based on Philippians 4:7: 'May the peace of God, which passes all understanding, guard your heart and your mind in Christ Jesus.'

Connecting with Scripture

- Jesus tells us not to worry about clothes, food or drink, but to trust that God knows what we need (Matthew 6:31–34).
- Paul reminds us not to be anxious about anything, but to pray and to receive God's peace, which transcends understanding (Philippians 4:6, 7).

Hand it Over

Young people may find this a helpful tool in their own times of prayer – to knot a string, and then to untangle it as they pray about each of the issues. Remind them that untying the knot is about choosing to trust God for that problem, rather than simplistically saying that the problem is now sorted. If they find it difficult to untie any of the knots, encourage them to talk about it to a friend, or someone they trust.

Body Language

WHAT HAPPENS?

Lead people in prayer and actions so that their body language mirrors what they are praying about.

EFFORT INVOLVED

MATERIALS NEEDED

Instrumental music to play in the background.

SOME THOUGHTS

Our lounge was full of boys lazing around watching football. Then suddenly England scored, and the space was transformed – a crush of bodies leapt up and down, shouting and laughing, hugging and punching each other, their delight obvious from their body language.

We can tell what people are feeling from the way they use their bodies, yet when we pray our posture often doesn't get beyond the 'shampoo position'. When we communicate so much with our bodies through most of our lives, why not also do it when we pray?

This exercise has a higher than usual potential for giggles to break out, so it needs a group with some maturity and willingness to give it a go. You may like to point out that David's wife, Michal, laughed at David's dancing, but what God saw was the sincerity of his heart, which was what really mattered (2 Samuel 6:16–23).

Talk about this experience afterwards and encourage people to use movement and appropriate body language in their own prayer as well. They could go for a walk or a run and pray, instead of sitting in their rooms. They could stand in front of the window and look out as they pray for their friends or neighbourhood. They could kneel or lie prostrate before God in praise and adoration. They could walk round the house and pray in the bedroom of each member of the family (maybe when everyone else is out of the house!).

HOW TO DO IT

Read the script below before the session and think about how to adapt it for your group. When you read the words (as adapted), leave pauses in appropriate places to allow people to do what the words suggest. You'll need to be aware of how people are responding, so won't be able to get lost in the experience yourself, but, as far as you can, lead the way by doing the actions yourself, or brief some other leaders or key young people so that they can engage fully.

Invite people to find a space in the room where they will be able to stretch out without touching other people. Explain that you're going to suggest physical movements for them to do during the prayer – kneeling, sitting, standing – and invite them to join in if they want to – but stress that they don't have to do anything that they don't feel comfortable about. You may want to encourage people to keep their eyes closed, or to suggest that people face a wall so that they aren't distracted by others.

> *Sit in your space and own it. This is your space to talk to God and to hear from God. As your body grows still, let your mind also settle; be still on the inside and still on the outside.*
> *Become aware of your breathing. Breathe slowly and deeply.*
> *Feel the air fill your lungs, and then swirl away as you breathe out.*
> *As you sit in God's presence, give thanks for God's love...*
> > *for God's acceptance of you...*
> > *for God's delight in you.*
> *You are loved... You are chosen... You are wanted... You belong.*

> *Now move your body so that you are kneeling before God.*
> *Place your hands on the floor in front of you and bow your head. Push down on the ground as you confess to God your brokenness: the things you wish you hadn't done; the things you know you should have done; the worries on your mind; the ways in which you have hurt others. Push down as you give these burdens to God.*

> *Then sit back on your heels. Lift your hands and turn your palms upwards. Sit with open hands to receive God's love and forgiveness.*
> *God forgives you... God accepts you... God loves you.*
> *Imagine that love, that forgiveness, that acceptance pouring into your open hands: overflowing, surrounding you, overwhelming you.*

> *Now stand in God's presence, tall and straight. Lift your head high, as a child of God. Stand in confidence and strength, secure in your Father's gaze.*
> *Lift your hands and praise the Lord. Give praise for who God is and what God has done.*

As your arms grow heavy, keep holding them up, to show how important God is to you. Sing out praise from your heart, from the depths of your being.

And then kneel again, as you bring your requests to God. Bow humbly before the Lord, as you talk to God about your needs and the needs of your friends.
    And finally sit again, as if you were at Jesus' feet. Enjoy his presence; feel the warmth of his smile.

Know that God has heard you.
Rest in God's presence.

Then invite people to bring their attention back to the room. You might close with some sung worship, or by saying the words of a prayer together.

CONNECTING WITH SCRIPTURE
- Moses lifted up his hands to God's throne when the Israelites were fighting the Amalekites (Exodus 17:11–13).
- David danced before the Lord because he was so pleased to see the ark of God back in Jerusalem (2 Samuel 6:14).
- Psalm 95:6 invites us to bow down in worship and kneel before God.
- Psalm 40:2 talks about God lifting David out of mud and mire and giving him a firm place to stand in confidence.
- Paul knelt in prayer before God (Ephesians 3:14).
- In a letter to Timothy, Paul wants men everywhere to lift up holy hands in prayer, rather than in anger or dispute (1 Timothy 2:8).

HAND IT OVER
Invite young people to create their own movements to the Lord's Prayer. They could work on this in small groups and then take it in turns to lead everyone else. Or invite them to create a set of movements that group members can use to help them find stillness in preparation for prayer.

Balloon Stomp

What Happens?

People write prayer requests on slips of paper, roll them up and put them into balloons, which are then blown up and batted around the room. On a signal, everyone bursts a balloon and prays for the request inside. Repeat until all the balloons are burst.

Effort Involved

Materials Needed

- Slips of paper
- Pens
- Three balloons for each person (or more)
- Upbeat praise music to accompany the prayer.

Some Thoughts

Usually corporate prayer is sedate, quiet and well-mannered – but it doesn't have to be! This activity is loud, chaotic and fun and may transform your group's experience of prayer.

How to Do it

Practice rolling up a slip of paper and inserting it into a balloon, so you know what size of paper works best. Prepare accordingly.

Think about how music could enhance this activity. You could get a band to play and lead worship during the prayer: people bat the balloons around during each verse of a song, and the worship leader instructs them to burst a balloon and pray in between. Or use a worship CD.

Invite people to write on slips of paper things that they want prayer for. You might suggest subjects for prayer – perhaps a friend in need, a global issue, a request for themselves – or just allow them free rein. They should roll up the piece of paper, insert it into the neck of a balloon, blow up the balloon and tie the neck. People can blow up as many balloons as they like – in fact, the more the better.

After about five minutes, when all the balloons are filled, each person hits the balloons they have filled up into the air and circulates them with all the others. Introduce the music you have planned. One or two people could stand on chairs and waft the balloons higher than people's heads. When you give the signal – by blowing a whistle, shouting, 'Go!', or pausing the music – each person grabs a balloon, stamps on it to burst it and reads the slip of paper inside. Then they pray out loud a short prayer for the issue. Allow a minute for this and then ask them to hit all the balloons up in the air again. On your signal, they grab another balloon, stamp on it, read the paper inside and pray as before. Repeat until all the balloons have been burst.

At the end, ask everyone to stand together. Lead a prayer thanking God that God has heard and will answer their prayers.

Alternative – Paper Aeroplanes

As an alternative, get people to write prayer requests on a piece of paper and then make it into a paper aeroplane. Everyone throws their aeroplane at the same time, then grabs the one that lands nearest to them and prays out loud for that person. Give a signal for everyone to make their piece of paper back into a plane and throw it again. Repeat the process several times, to give people plenty of opportunities to pray for one another.

Or get people to write a blessing on their paper before turning it into an aeroplane. Launch the planes and then invite each person to take away a blessing as they leave the session or service. You could do this at a service where people are leaving to go to university or college. Invite everyone in the congregation to write a blessing or prayer for the future student life of these young people. Then, as you pray, invite everyone to launch their aeroplanes in a shower of blessings. Collect them up and share them among the students to take away with them.

Connecting with Scripture

- There are no balloons in the Bible, but several times the Psalms encourage shouts of joy in God's presence (Psalms 20:5; 27:6; 33:3).
- Ezra describes a chaotic scene when the foundations of the temple were laid in Jerusalem. Some shouted for joy, some wept, and it was hard to work out who was doing what (Ezra 3:10–13).

Hand it Over

Invite people to think about other ways in which they can set the tone of a prayer session through the use of movement, activity, music or visuals.

Lifted

What Happens?

The group lift people physically as they pray for them, to symbolize the way our prayer upholds and supports each other.

Effort Involved

Materials Needed

None, unless it is easier to lift people on a blanket or something else (see below).

Some Thoughts

It requires trust to allow others to lift you up; but then, it requires trust to allow others to pray for you. Getting people to enact physically what is happening spiritually as we pray for one another can be enlightening and profound.

How to Do it

This is best done in a group of between 10 and 30 people, so you have enough people to take it in turns to lift someone, but not too many, so that some people are only looking on. You need to be aware of health and safety issues, of course. Only allow one person to be lifted at a time, so that you can supervise what's going on. And watch for gender issues – you don't want guys feeling uncomfortable because the girls lifting them have their hands in inappropriate places, or vice versa! You could get people to lie on a blanket or a camp bed and lift that instead, if you feel it's more appropriate.

Introduce the idea and invite people to share things that they would like prayer for. It may help to have spoken to someone in advance, who will then be willing to be lifted first. Encourage people to pray as they lift the person, out loud or silently; you may like to 'top and tail' the time by starting and closing in prayer. Let the person be held up for long enough for people to feel the strain in their arms, to make people aware of the effort and endurance that is needed in prayer. With a larger group, rotate those who are physically doing the lifting, so that everyone has a go. You may want to encourage people to keep their eyes open so that they can be aware if anyone is getting into difficulties!

CONNECTING WITH SCRIPTURE

- Jesus wanted the support and presence of his friends while he prayed in anguish in the Garden of Gethsemane (Matthew 26:36–46).
- Paul invites his friends to join in his struggle by praying for him (Romans 15:30).

Maps

What Happens?

On a map of the local area, people put fingerprints on key places that they regularly visit as they pray for them.

Effort Involved

Materials Needed

- A map of the local area
- Inkpads
- Wipes to clean fingers
- Bin for discarded wipes.

Some Thoughts

Sometimes there seems little connection between our worship at church and the rest of our lives. Safe inside the walls of the church, we have little to remind us that we spend the vast majority of our week living, working and studying among people who need to experience the love of God. This activity is a way of recording the places we connect with on a regular basis in the local area, through our homes, our schools, our leisure, our work, our shopping and so on – and praying for them.

How to Do it

Choose a map off your local area. If people travel from a wide area to your group, it may be more difficult to find a map that will be relevant to everyone. If that's the case, you can get people to attach sticky notes to the edges, with arrows or comments about their connections to places outside the boundaries of the map. Lay the map on the floor with the inkpads around the edge, and get people to gather round.

You could lead people through praying for different places. Invite them to pray for their homes – for their families and their immediate neighbours, placing a fingerprint on the appropriate place as they do so. Then get them to pray for their schools and colleges – again marking the map with their fingerprints as they pray – and so on, focusing in turn on work, leisure, church, or friends' houses as appropriate.

Keep the map after the activity as a visual reminder of the group's connections to the local area and of their prayer.

ALTERNATIVE – GLOBAL ISSUES

You can also do this activity on a global scale, getting people to put fingerprints on a world map and pray for countries around the world. This works best if there's a theme – perhaps praying for people working in mission in other countries, or places in the news in the last week, or areas of conflict.

ALTERNATIVE – NIGHTLIGHTS ON A MAP

Another now familiar idea is to get people to light nightlights as they pray and to place them on a map. Each nightlight will need to be placed in a holder for safety. This is a wonderful visual reminder of Jesus being the light of the world (John 8:12), and in turn calling us the light of the world (Matthew 5:14).

ALTERNATIVE – UV ROUTES

Invite people to draw on the map a route that they take to school/college/work – or to mark the places where they live, study and work – using a UV pen of the type used for security marking. The results will be invisible under normal light. Later in the service, turn on a UV light near the map. The routes that people have traced on it will show up, revealing the presence of the body of Christ in your city or town. You can use this as an impetus for prayer – that God would be revealed, that the presence of God would be felt, that we would take seriously Jesus' words that we are the light of the world (Matthew 5:14). Do an internet search for 'UV strip light' or 'UV blacklight' to find suppliers of the UV lights.

CONNECTING WITH SCRIPTURE

- The exiles in Babylon were called to seek the peace and prosperity of the city in which they were living and to pray for it (Jeremiah 29:7).
- Jesus challenges us to be a neighbour to those in need around us (Luke 10:25–37).

HAND IT OVER

Encourage people to think about how they can love and serve people in those places, as well as praying for them. They got their hands dirty placing fingerprints on the map; can they get their hands dirty engaging in their neighbourhood?

Ancestors of Faith

What Happens?

People use wire to 'write' other people's names and hang them on a tree branch,[1] as a way of thanking God for those who have been significant in our journey of faith.

Effort Involved

Materials Needed

- A tree branch or two
- A Christmas-tree stand, or a pot with soil or stones, to hold the tree branches upright
- Florists' wire, thin and plastic-coated
- Secateurs or strong scissors to cut the wire
- You may like to play some instrumental music during this activity.

Some Thoughts

Spend a few moments talking to someone about how their relationship with Jesus developed, and they will tell you about the people who played a significant role in their lives: the older woman in church who used to pray for them; the Sunday-school teacher who still keeps in touch; the friend who challenged them about their faith; or the student who set a good example. This is an opportunity to acknowledge the role that those people have played, to thank God for them and to pray for them in return.

How to Do it

Cut the wire into lengths of about 1 metre. Set the tree branches into a stand, so that they are held securely and won't topple over.

Invite people to think about their Christian 'family tree': the people who introduced them to Jesus, or who prayed for them, or who have given them advice and support. Invite them to choose one person and to make their name, using the wire, to hang on the tree while they give thanks for them and pray for them in return.

People need to bend the wire to 'write' the person's name, creating

---

1   Mike Rose

letters in 'joined-up' writing. You may like to make one or two examples to show people how it can be done.

You could invite people to say a few words about the person they want to give thanks for as they add their name to the tree. Keep a prayerful atmosphere during the creating of the names, as well as when they are added to the tree.

Invite people to spend a few moments looking at the names on the tree. These people have been significant in our lives; who are the people that God is calling us to do the same for? Who can we pray for, encourage, support? In ten or twenty years' time, who are the people who will be putting our names on another tree? Pray that you will all have opportunities to encourage others in their faith, to pass on the support that you have been given. Invite people to think intentionally about who they can pray for.

Alternative – In Memory

This activity could have a focus on people who have died, giving people an opportunity to thank God for their lives and to ask for God's comfort in their grief. This may work best as part of an activity for the wider church that some young people help to plan and can go to if they want to.

Alternative – Footsteps on the Journey[2]

Run a length of lining paper down the central aisle of the church, or from one side of the room to the other. Invite people to draw round one of their feet on the paper, so that all the feet are pointing in the same direction. Invite people to write in on their footprint the names of people who have been significant in their journey of faith, and to pray for them, giving thanks. This is a good all-age activity.

Connecting with Scripture

- Several times, Paul urges Christians to follow his example – see 1 Corinthians 11:1, for example. Are we confident enough in our faith to say the same to others?
- Timothy learned from the example of his mother Eunice and grandmother Lois (2 Timothy 1:5).
- The writer of Hebrews reminds us of the great cloud of witnesses: the people who have gone before us in our faith (Hebrews 11).

---

2 Anna Poulson

HAND IT OVER

Give some of the young people an opportunity to create names out of wire before the session, so that they can help others during it.

A simpler version that young people may like to lead themselves is to cut leaf shapes out of paper, write names on them and attach them with string to the tree branches. Or they can draw a tree trunk on a large sheet of paper and invite people to add names on leaves to complete the tree while they pray.

They could use the 'writing with wire' idea to identify other things that they would like prayer for – the characteristics they would like to develop, or the fruit of the Spirit that they want to see grow in their lives. If you have space to leave the tree on display where your group meets, it will remind them of the things they have prayed for.

Burdens

What Happens?

People carry weights to represent burdens of worry or sin, and then have an opportunity to pray for each other.

Effort Involved

Materials Needed

- A bag for each person – this could be a strong paper bag, a plastic carrier bag, a backpack or a small duffel bag
- Weights, such as bricks, potatoes or stones – allow four or five for each person
- A cross or altar – a place where people can leave their burdens
- A length of coloured ribbon about 10 centimetres long and a small gold safety pin for each person
- Worshipful music to play during the activity.

Some Thoughts

Talking about problems can help put things into perspective and take a load off your mind. Praying about them involves God, who can give real peace and bring about lasting change. This activity helps people to identify what is weighing them down and then pray about those things with a friend. Sometimes it is only when we start to pray about issues that we realize just how much of a burden they have been to us. Prayer doesn't always offer instant solutions, and so people will take away a reminder to continue to pray for each other.

How to Do It

Have a pile of bags at the door, so that each person can collect one as they enter. Put a pile of weights – bricks, potatoes or stones – in a central place. Choose an appropriate place for people to leave their burdens – at the altar at the front of the church, or at the foot of a cross. Leave the lengths of ribbon and the safety pins there.

Invite people to think about the things that are weighing them down at the moment – worries, unconfessed sin, damaged relationships, or stress. They should collect a weight to represent each care and add it to their bag. Ask them to walk around the church or room for three or four minutes, feeling the weight of their burdens; play some suitable music during this.

Then ask people to pair up, stand together and take it in turns to pray for each other. The person who is going to listen and pray first can put down their own bag for the time being. The person who is to be prayed for should hold onto their bag and talk about what the weights represent. The two people should then pray together: for situations to be resolved; for God's provision; for forgiveness. Together, they then take the weights to the front of the church or to the foot of the cross and leave them there. The person who has listened and prayed should take a piece of ribbon and pin it on, to remind them to keep praying for their partner. Allow five to ten minutes for this discussion and prayer, and let people know when they have a minute left.

Then they swap roles – the second person talks about what their weights represent and the first person prays for them. Together they then take these burdens to the front of the church. Again, allow about fifteen minutes for this prayer to take place. The relief of letting go of the bags is very real after you have been holding them for a while!

Close with some sung worship, or a responsive prayer that people can join in.

Connecting with Scripture

- If we confess our sins, God forgives us – simple as that. Sometimes the burden that we carry, though, is our inability to forgive ourselves and to move into the freedom that God has for us (1 John 1:9).
- Paul encourages us to carry one another's burdens (Galatians 6:2).

Praying Out Loud

WHAT HAPPENS?

Provide a structure for people to write prayers and then to read them out, to get over their fears of praying out loud.

EFFORT INVOLVED

MATERIALS NEEDED

- Pens and paper
- Words of response for people to join in (see below): copy the sheet on page 38, or project the words using an overhead projector or data projector
- You may like to play some worship music in the background.

SOME THOUGHTS

I didn't pray out loud in a group until I was 18 and at university. Dragged to an early-morning missionary prayer meeting by a friend, I was horrified to discover that everyone present was given a situation to pray for, and that we were all expected to pray out loud. If you didn't voice your prayer, then your missionary would lose out, and who knows what might have happened! I stumbled out an awkward prayer, having rehearsed it 5,000 times in my head while everyone else was praying, and I survived. Since then I've got used to it, and can trot out as much Christianized prayer-language jargon as the next person, but I've never forgotten that first experience.

This is a very simple idea, but it's included to help people over that hurdle of speaking prayer aloud in front of others. The longer people in your group stay quiet in group prayer times, the harder it will be to join in. This activity helps them to use their voices – to try out what they sound like in the context of prayer – without the added terror of thinking up some good words to say on the spot.

But I would also want to challenge the assumption that unspoken prayer is not 'real' prayer. God hears the cries of our heart, whether they are spoken aloud or kept to ourselves; whether they are phrased in coherent sentences or are scattered thoughts; whether they just really include the right jargon, or are authentic to the way that we normally speak.

So see this as a way of equipping those who want to pray out loud but need a bit of help, rather than forcing everyone into the same mode of expression, and try to communicate that in the way you introduce the activity.

How to Do it

Explain that you're going to pray together a bit differently, and you're going to give people a chance to think about what they want to say. Invite people to take paper and pen and find a space where they are comfortable.

Invite people to think of things that they want to thank God for – it could be something that's happened this week, something they've received, a person they are grateful for... Invite them to write it down and explain that they will have a chance to read it out in a few moments. Give them space to think and write.

Then invite people to think about something that they want to say sorry to God for – perhaps something they said, something they thought, or something they did that they regret. Invite them to write down something that they will be comfortable to read out in a few minutes. They don't have to go into details if they don't want to; God will know what they mean. Give them space to think and write.

Finally, invite people to think of something that they want to ask God for – perhaps a friend who is in need, or a situation in the world, or something more personal. Again, invite them to write down something that they will be comfortable to read out. Give them space to think and write.

Then invite people to sit round in a circle. Hand out the words that you're going to use, or make sure that everyone can see them. Explain that in the 'time to say thank you', they are going to take it in turns to read out their prayers of thanks around the circle – make sure they know who will start off, and which way round the circle the turns will go. Similarly, in the time to say sorry and the time to pray they will read out the other prayers they have written. It's best to follow the same pattern of who reads first and which way round the circle you go, so that people feel secure about what is happening.

Then read the lines on the sheet and invite people to join in the responses printed in bold. Using their voices alongside everyone else will give them confidence to speak on their own. Keep the whole activity prayerful. You could end with a prayer, thanking God that God has heard all the cries of their hearts, spoken and unspoken.

Connecting with Scripture

Jesus taught that God listens to the cries of our heart, rather than whether we use impressive words or actions (Luke 18:9–14).

Hand it Over

Encourage people to form prayer triplets and to meet together to pray for one another. A small group of good friends is an excellent context in which to try out your praying-out-loud skills.

Give people practice in public speaking and teach them some skills, so that they are able to lead written prayers in services or in your youth group. Don't just assume that they'll be able to do it.

Join in the words printed in bold.

Why have you come here?
We have come to worship Jesus.

What do you bring with you?
All that we are – our joy and pain, our ideas and worries.

What will you do here?
We will draw close to Jesus.

You are welcome.
Jesus is here.
Receive his love.
Offer your praise.

A time to say 'Thank you'...

Jesus, we have tried to follow you,
But sometimes we have failed.
We have done things we shouldn't have done.
We have not done things we should have done.
We need your forgiveness,
And so we come to say sorry.

A time to say 'Sorry'...

Jesus has heard your confession.
You are forgiven.
You can move on in peace.

Jesus said:
'Ask and it will be given to you; seek and you will find;
knock and the door will be opened to you.'
We can come to Jesus with all that's on our hearts,
knowing that he loves us;
knowing that he hears us;
knowing that he will respond.

A time to pray...

Feed on God

WHAT HAPPENS?

People write words from Bible verses in icing on cupcakes or biscuits and give them to friends to eat, encouraging them to feed on God's words.

EFFORT INVOLVED

MATERIALS NEEDED

- Plain cupcakes or plain biscuits, home-made or bought
- Icing sugar and colourings, to make icing
- Tubes of icing for writing, or nozzles and icing bags, or greaseproof paper
- Bowls for mixing
- Accompanying sheet of Bible verses, or your own alternative
- Worship music to play in the background.

SOME THOUGHTS

We're all very aware of healthy eating these days. It may not actually affect what we put in our mouths, but we know that we need to eat more fruit and vegetables, less fat, less sugar, fewer processed foods... Our physical health depends in part on what we put into our bodies.

Similarly, our spiritual health depends in part on what we take into our hearts and minds. The Bible talks about God's words being sweet as honey. Will we feed on the truth of God's word?

HOW TO DO IT

Choose a focus for the Bible texts that you will use in this activity. You could use verses from Psalm 103, for example, where David calls to mind all the benefits that the Lord brings him. Or you could get people to choose words and phrases from Ephesians 1:1–14, a fantastically rich passage on the reality of our relationship with God. The words on the accompanying page are from the Sermon on the Mount in Matthew 5–7, which give people a chance to feed on the challenging words of Jesus.

Explain the activity. Talk about the need for us to feed on God's word: to take in the truth of what God has said so that it becomes part of who we are. Explain that you're going to give people space to meditate on a

Bible verse, and then to write a word or phrase from it on a cake or biscuit using icing. They should meditate on the Bible text as they create their cake, repeating some of the words to themselves and thinking about how it applies to them.

Hand out the Bible verses on slips of paper (you could use Bibles, but they might well get sticky!) and show people the materials. Encourage an atmosphere of worship and reflection. People won't be able to write a whole verse on each cake or biscuit, so they should choose a phrase or word or image, or maybe decorate several cakes or biscuits to communicate their verse.

Once the cakes are decorated, invite people to choose someone to give their cake to, along with the slip of paper that the verse was written on. This could be part of the worship, or they could take them away with them to give to someone not present. They should invite the recipient to eat the cake while reading the text and meditating on God's word.

ALTERNATIVE – RICE PAPER TEXTS

You could get people to write prayers or blessings on rice paper, using pens with edible ink, and then give these to others to eat. Or, during a 'stations' style of service, have ready a Bible text that you want people to focus on, written on rice paper, and invite people to read it and then eat it, to symbolize their intention to be nourished by it. You can get pens with edible ink from cake-decorating websites or shops. To find these, search on the internet for 'edible ink pens'.

CONNECTING WITH SCRIPTURE

- Psalm 19 says that God's words are sweeter than honey from the honeycomb (Psalm 19:7–10).
- Ezekiel was given a scroll of God's words to eat before he went to speak to the house of Israel (Ezekiel 3:1–3).
- Paul encourages Timothy to be nourished by the teaching he has received (1 Timothy 4:6).
- Paul tells us to dwell on what is true, noble, right and pure (Philippians 4:8).

HAND IT OVER

Involve people in making the cakes and biscuits in advance of the session or service where you plan to use them. Baking is a useful skill and a great group activity, but also encourage them to view the baking as part of the worship.

You are the salt of the earth. But if the salt loses its saltiness, how can it be made salty again? It is no longer good for anything, except to be thrown out and trampled underfoot.
Matthew 5:13

You are the light of the world. A city on a hill cannot be hidden. Neither do people light a lamp and put it under a bowl. Instead they put it on its stand, and it gives light to everyone in the house. In the same way, let your light shine before others, that they may see your good deeds and praise your Father in heaven.
Matthew 5:14–16

When you give to the needy, do not let your left hand know what your right hand is doing, so that your giving may be in secret. Then your Father, who sees what is done in secret, will reward you.
Matthew 6:3, 4

For if you forgive others when they sin against you, your heavenly Father will also forgive you. But if you do not forgive others their sins, your Father will not forgive your sins.
Matthew 6:14, 15

Do not store up for yourselves treasures on earth, where moth and rust destroy, and where thieves break in and steal. But store up for yourselves treasures in heaven, where moth and rust do not destroy, and where thieves do not break in and steal. For where your treasure is, there your heart will be also.
Matthew 6:19–21

The eye is the lamp of the body. If your eyes are healthy, your whole body will be full of light. But if your eyes are unhealthy, your whole body will be full of darkness. If then the light within you is darkness, how great is that darkness!
Matthew 6:22–23

No one can be a loyal servant to two masters. Either you will hate the one and love the other, or you will be devoted to the one and despise the other. You cannot faithfully serve both God and Money.
Matthew 6:24

Therefore I tell you, do not worry about your life, what you will eat or drink; or about your body, what you will wear. Is not life more important than food, and the body more important than clothes? Look at the birds of the air; they do not sow or reap or store away in barns, and yet your heavenly Father feeds them. Are you not much more valuable than they? Can any one of you by worrying add a single hour to your life?
Matthew 6:25–27

Do not judge, or you too will be judged. For in the same way you judge others, you will be judged, and with the measure you use, it will be measured to you.
Matthew 7:1–2

Ask and it will be given to you; seek and you will find; knock and the door will be opened to you. For everyone who asks receives; those who seek find; and to those who knock, the door will be opened.
Matthew 7:7–8

Which of you, if your son asks for bread, will give him a stone? Or if he asks for a fish, will give him a snake? If you, then, though you are evil, know how to give good gifts to your children, how much more will your Father in heaven give good gifts to those who ask him!
Matthew 7:9–11

Enter through the narrow gate. For wide is the gate and broad is the road that leads to destruction, and many enter through it. But small is the gate and narrow the road that leads to life, and only a few find it.
Matthew 7:13–14

Therefore everyone who hears these words of mine and puts them into practice is like a wise man who built his house on the rock. The rain came down, the streams rose, and the winds blew and beat against that house; yet it did not fall, because it had its foundation on the rock. But everyone who hears these words of mine and does not put them into practice is like a foolish man who built his house on sand. The rain came down, the streams rose, and the winds blew and beat against that house, and it fell with a great crash.
Matthew 7:24–27

Rhythm of Prayer

What Happens?

People receive text messages three times a day, reminding them to pray.

Effort Involved

Materials Needed

- Young people with mobile phones
- A web-based SMS service, for example www.sms2email.co.uk

Some Thoughts

A couple of years ago I went on retreat to Burford Priory, a Benedictine community. Six times a day, the monks and nuns gathered in the wood-panelled chapel for worship, starting at 6:45 am for Lauds and ending with Compline at 9pm. Each day has a rhythm of prayer and worship that sets a framework for everything else that is done. It was interesting to be a part of that rhythm: to realize that God was being worshipped so faithfully by this community and to be drawn into that.

Many young people find it difficult to sustain their relationship with God outside of youth group meetings, especially if they don't have Christian friends at school or Christian family members. Using this idea for a season will remind them that they are part of the wider body of Christ and will help them to make prayer a regular part of their day.

This will be an exclusive activity if some of your group don't have mobile phones, so only use it if all of your group have access to them. Texting prayers lends itself nicely to call and response – you text 'The Lord be with you,' and they text back 'And also with you' – but, again, I'd suggest you don't use this idea during this activity, as it could be prohibitively expensive for some.

How to Do it

Investigate web-based SMS services that enable you to send one message to lots of phone numbers online.

Decide what period of time this activity will cover – a week? A fortnight? Then choose appropriate times of day. If most of them are at school during the week, where mobile phones are banned, you won't want to send lunchtime text messages. You could choose first thing in the morning, after school and then last thing at night. Be considerate of teenage sleep patterns and make your first text later at the weekends, if you still want them to be speaking to you by the end of the exercise.

Invite people to sign up to be part of this. The idea is that, when they get the text, they pause for a moment to pray, guided by the words they have just received. Encourage them to remember that the rest of the group will be praying at the same time.

Here are some suggestions for what you could text over the course of a week. You could include a short Bible verse or encouragement to focus on God, as well as a suggestion for something to pray for.

Morning Texts – Focus on Praising God
- *Monday:* God has been watching over you during the night. Thank God that God is with you.
- *Tuesday:* God's love is new every morning. Remind yourself that God loves you!
- *Wednesday:* From the rising of the sun to the place where it sets, God's name is praised. Start your day by praising God.
- *Thursday:* God wipes away your sins like the morning mist. Thank God for God's forgiveness. Today is a fresh start.
- *Friday:* Look at the world around you; God created all this and God made you. Give praise to your Creator.
- *Saturday:* Jesus said we should ask God for our daily bread. Thank God for all that God provides for you.
- *Sunday:* Jesus rose from the dead on a Sunday morning. How did that change the world? Praise God that Jesus is alive.

Early Evening Texts – Focus on Praying for People
- *Monday:* Draw near to God and God will draw near to you. Tell God what's on your heart.
- *Tuesday:* God will give good gifts to those who ask God. Pray for your best friend.
- *Wednesday:* Keep on praying for all God's people. Take time to pray for your family.
- *Thursday:* You are part of the body of Christ here on earth. Pray for someone in your youth group.
- *Friday:* Seek the peace and prosperity of the city where you live. Pray for your town or city, for people to know God.

- *Saturday:* Jesus is the Prince of Peace. Pray for a place in the world where there is conflict.
- *Sunday:* God loved the world so much that God sent Jesus. Pray for a place in the world where people are in need.

Night Texts – Reflect on the Day that has Been, or the One to Come
- *Monday:* Think back over today. Is there anything you regret? Talk to God about it. Receive God's forgiveness.
- *Tuesday:* Think back over today. What are you most grateful for? Tell God about it.
- *Wednesday:* Think about tomorrow. Are you worried about anything? Give that worry to God, who loves you.
- *Thursday:* Think about the people you met. Who made you happy? Thank God for them, and tell them tomorrow.
- *Friday:* Think about the people you met. Did any friendships go wrong? Talk to God about it. Decide to put things right tomorrow.
- *Saturday:* Think about your family. How do you feel about them? Tell God, and ask for God's help to love and serve them.
- *Sunday:* How do you feel about next week? Tell God about it, and thank God that God will be with you through it, whatever happens.

ALTERNATIVE – BIBLE STUDY
Use this idea to study a Bible passage together over the course of a week. Text the participants a verse or two, with a question to reflect on, three times a day. Then, during your youth group session they will hopefully have questions and thoughts to contribute to a discussion of that same passage.

CONNECTING WITH SCRIPTURE
- David cries out to God morning, noon and night, confident that he will be heard (Psalm 55:17).
- David thinks of God through the structure of the night watches – three sentry duties that took place during the night (Psalm 63:6).
- While this idea won't get you praying continually, as Paul exhorts in 1 Thessalonians 5:17, it may help you to pray more regularly for a season!

Hand it Over

Get a small group of young people to help you to set this up. Consult with them about what times to send the texts. Get them to write prayers and so on.

People could also use this idea to encourage one another in prayer, texting prayers to each other at key moments of the day. Or they could set alarms on their watches to remind them to pray at certain times, knowing that others will also be praying then.

CHAPTER 2

Worship

These ideas are designed to be used during a time when people gather for worship, whether that's in a church service, at a youth group, or more informally. Some give the outline of a single activity that could be used during a longer service, or to provide a worship focus at the end of a session. Others give a variety of activities and words that can be used to create a whole service on a particular theme.

However you use these ideas, you need to think about the structure and flow of the worship service: how people will move from the busyness of their lives into an awareness of God's presence and a place where they can hear and receive from God. As a creator of worship, the environment you construct using music, visuals, lighting and seating will be one element that encourages people to be open and receptive to God. Also important are the words you use, the example you show, the way that you speak about God and the space that you leave for people to reflect and respond.

One of the paradoxes of gathered worship is that it is both corporate and individual. We worship together as the people of God, but we also respond to God out of the unique contexts of our individual lives. Worship that focuses too much on the corporate experience can be alienating or false for those who are at a different place in their own lives. Worship that focuses too much on the individual can be subjective and inward-looking. Well-structured worship acknowledges that both are taking place and skilfully weaves them together.

Mosaic

WHAT HAPPENS?

People write their disappointments and failures on pieces of coloured paper. They tear these up into small pieces and use them to make a mosaic picture.

EFFORT INVOLVED

MATERIALS NEEDED

- A large sheet of paper
- Small sheets of coloured paper, of many different shades and textures
- Plenty of glue sticks
- Plenty of pens
- Instrumental music to play in the background.

SOME THOUGHTS

First Presbyterian Church, Lisburn, contains a beautiful stained-glass window known as the Resurrection Window. It was created out of fragments of coloured glass that had been blown out of the original windows at the church during the height of the troubles in Northern Ireland. The congregation decided to stay at the church building and rebuild it, as a witness to their hope for peace in their country. The Resurrection Window has a spiral of glass at its centre that portrays a new sort of explosion – of God's power to bring peace and reconciliation. And it's a powerful picture of the way in which God can bring beauty out of brokenness and order out of chaos.

God delights to take our brokenness and turn it into something beautiful and useful. Where some people might see failure or missed opportunities, God sees the potential for grace and healing. Instead of being crippled by disappointment and rejection, we are invited by God to learn from it and move on.

HOW TO DO IT

This idea works best if you have one or two people to direct the making of the mosaic. They should sketch out a basic design on the large sheet of paper. The mosaic directors can write in pencil what colour each section should be and start the picture off by sticking on some pieces of paper to show people how to do it. Mosaics can have small spaces left between the pieces of paper – where the grouting would go if the mosaic was made of tiles – or the pieces can be stuck directly next to each other, which is the technique used with *smalti*, pieces of brightly coloured Italian glass.

Then, as people come to stick their small pieces of paper on the sheet, the mosaic directors can guide the placing of the pieces and add any extra pieces as seems necessary. They are there not to take over, but to help people feel more secure. Have the coloured paper and pens in small piles around the room, so that they are easily accessible. Have lots of glue sticks by the mosaic picture, so that several people can stick their pieces on at once.

Invite everybody to collect a piece of coloured paper and think about any brokenness and disappointment in their lives – times when they have let others down, or feel God has let them down, or things have gone wrong. They should write these on one side of the paper. Then they tear the paper into little pieces to symbolize the brokenness as they pray and ask God to come to them in their hurt. The pieces don't have to be squares.

Invite people to take their pieces of paper and add them to the mosaic picture using the glue sticks. It will take time to build the picture up, but this will enable people to have plenty of space to pray, on their own or for one another. You could encourage people to talk in pairs about what they have put on the paper and pray for each other. Make sure everyone has a chance to add at least some of their pieces to the mosaic.

If the mosaic is not finished by the time this part of the service needs to end, lift it up so that everyone can see what it looks like so far. As a 'work in progress', an unfinished mosaic is perhaps a very appropriate symbol of God's work in our lives! Lead everyone in thanking God that God is with them in their brokenness and praying that God will continue to create beauty from pain and disappointment. Invite people to stay afterwards and help finish the mosaic, if appropriate, or ask the mosaic directors to finish it during the week. Once it is completed, the picture can be displayed in the room where you meet, or the church.

CONNECTING WITH SCRIPTURE

God promises to give us beauty in place of ashes, the oil of joy for mourning and a garment of praise instead of a spirit of despair (Isaiah 61:3).

HAND IT OVER

Get a couple of young people to be the 'mosaic directors' for this activity, planning the structure of the picture in advance and gently guiding people where to place their pieces of paper.

Wailing Wall

What Happens?

People are given space to express their complaints to God on a graffiti wall. They have an opportunity to take away a portion of the wall and make a choice to wait for God.[3]

Effort Involved

Materials Needed

- A roll of lining paper
- Pens and paints
- Angry music to play in the background.

Some Thoughts

There's a tradition within the Jewish faith of complaining to God. It's not something that most of us find easy. Maybe it's something to do with being British; or maybe it's because we somehow feel we need to be on our best behaviour before God. And yet the Bible contains many complaints against God, in Psalms, Ecclesiastes, Lamentations and Job. The message of these books is that it's OK to tell God exactly how we feel. God is big enough to cope and, somehow, expressing our complaints and angst can help us to see them more objectively.

But it's also important for us to leave with hope in God, and that's where Lamentations is really helpful. Jeremiah doesn't hold back from saying what he thinks about God – 'he has broken my teeth with gravel; he has trampled me in the dust'(3:16) – but after offloading all that, he consciously calls to mind God's goodness and declares his intention to wait for God (3:19–24).

How to Do it

You'll probably want to do this activity in response to a mood of complaint or struggle that you have sensed in your group, or after an event like a natural disaster, when people are finding it hard to work out where God is, rather than springing it on a group from 'cold'. You don't

---

3 Clare Birch, Sanctuary

want people to feel they have to invent complaints against God when they don't have any!

Set up a long piece of paper on one wall, sticking together two or three strips of lining paper if necessary. If you are using paints, cover the floor with newspaper to protect it. Invite everyone to find something to write with and a space on the wall, and to write out or draw their complaints and honest feelings to God. You may want to play some angry music while you do this.

When people have had enough time to write, gradually fade out the music. Allow a few moments of calm, and then read these verses from Lamentations 3:19–26:

> *I remember my affliction and my wandering,*
> *the bitterness and the gall.*
> *I well remember them,*
> *and my soul is downcast within me.*
> *Yet this I call to mind*
> *and therefore I have hope:*

> *Because of the Lord's great love we are not consumed,*
> *for his compassions never fail.*
> *They are new every morning;*
> *great is your faithfulness.*
> *I say to myself, 'The Lord is my portion;*
> *therefore I will wait for him.'*

> *The Lord is good to those whose hope is in him,*
> *to the one who seeks him;*
> *it is good to wait quietly*
> *for the salvation of the Lord.*

Invite people to join you in taking down the wall. They have voiced their complaints, and God has heard them. They don't need to linger in that place, but are invited to move on. Invite people to tear out a small piece of the wall in the shape of the cross and write on it, 'I will wait for God.'

Pray on behalf of the group, thanking God that God has heard their cries, and that God's mercies are new every morning. Encourage people to take their cross away with them, to remind them that they can always be honest with God.

Connecting with Scripture

- Jeremiah speaks his lament to God honestly and clearly, but also calls to mind God's goodness and his intent to wait for God (Lamentations 3:1–33).
- The writer of Psalm 88 is completely in despair, without even a glimmer of faith and hope, and blames God for it.

Hand it Over

Encourage people to keep a journal in which they write down their thoughts and feelings, honestly and in secret. It's a good tool for reflection and can help people to track God's action in their lives.

Spirit

What Happens?

People are blindfolded and take part in a sensory journey into a worship experience, to mirror our need to be awake to the Spirit of God, whom we cannot see.[4]

Effort Involved

Materials Needed

- Blindfolds: those provided on long-haul flights are ideal, or use scarves
- Plain stickers for name badges
- Pens
- Materials to create the multi-sensory walk – see suggestions below
- CDs or MP3s and players to create the white-noise space
- Music, images and words to provide food for thought in the worship space.

Some Thoughts

I have come to really appreciate the rhythm of the church year and the opportunity it provides to celebrate the seasons of Advent, Christmas, Lent, Easter and Pentecost. It means that we need to be creative in finding different ways to explore similar themes year after year.

This service grew from the invisibility of God's Spirit. We cannot see the Spirit; we need to be awake to the Spirit's presence in other ways. I'll describe what we did, as a catalyst for your own imagination. We set up a multi-sensory walk down the side of our church that people would undertake blindfolded. They walked over stones, felt the windows and the brick of the wall of the church and walked past heaters and cut lemons. At the end of the church they entered a space of white noise, where they were spun round to disorientate them. Then someone called their name and invited them to walk forward into the worship space, where they could take off their blindfolds.

Other ideas for worship on the theme of the Spirit are given here.

---

4 Eirwen Dorkins, Ben Cohen and Gwen Page helped to develop these ideas.

How to Do it

Choose the space you will use for your multi-sensory walk. Set it up along a wall, so that people can guide themselves with one hand on the wall as they walk. Think about what people will feel, sense and smell while they walk.

- *Underfoot:* We used slate chippings from the garden; a thick blanket; some clear Perspex; a pilates mat; a large cardboard box; and a door-mat. You will need to secure these to the floor with gaffer tape, to make sure people don't slip or trip.
- *Along the wall:* It works well if your wall is textured, but you can also add bubble wrap; crunched-up silver foil; a soft bathmat; or fur fabric.
- *Smells:* At one end of the walk we had a plate of lemons and oranges that we had cut and partly squeezed just before the walk started. At the other we had a perfumed oil burner, lit; or you could use a scented candle.
- *Warmth:* Halfway along the walk we had a fan heater blowing out warm air.

Once this walk is set up, get someone who has not seen what is there to try it out, so that you can see if there are any hazards!

At the end of the walk create a space with disorientating noise. You could record some white noise from an untuned radio, or get someone to create something using a music-editing program, or play two or three different tracks at the same time.

It will take a while for everyone to enter the worship space by this route, so think about what people will find to do while they are waiting for other people to enter.

You will need a number of volunteers to help facilitate the walk:

- One or two people to set participants off on the walk. You need people to gather outside the worship space, where they can't see the walk before they take part in it. The volunteers will greet participants, ask them to take their shoes off and put on a blindfold. They also need to make sure that each person is wearing a sticker with their name on. They should send people on the walk at intervals, so that participants don't catch each other up.

- One or two people to greet participants at the other end and spin them round to disorientate them. They may also need to ask participants to wait, if people have caught up with one another.
- One person to call people by name into the worship space. They should stand in front of the participant, who is still in the white-noise space, and say something like: 'Jacob, come this way. Walk towards me.' They may need to be persistent, but should try to get the participant to take a step without being touched.
- Some people to provide music, images and words that people can reflect on once they get into the worship space. You could project Bible passages about the Spirit, or images of Spirit metaphors; or give people Bible passages with questions, to discuss in groups, or art materials with which to draw their own metaphors for the Spirit.

Once everyone had arrived in the worship space, we used these words, followed by the prayer below (see 'Alternative – Spirit Prayer').

> *Jesus said: 'The wind blows wherever it pleases. You hear its sound, but you cannot tell where it comes from or where it is going. So it is with everyone born of the Spirit.'*
>
> *We cannot see the Spirit of God with our eyes, so we need to use different ways to sense the presence of the Spirit. We hope your journey into the service tonight awoke your senses other than your sight. What was that experience like?*
>
> *How often are we aware of the Spirit of God? We are so used to our busyness – to the tangible, demanding world we live in – that we forget to tune in to the presence of God.*

You will then need to think about how your service will progress. What else will people learn about the Spirit? What opportunities will they have to respond to the Spirit?

ALTERNATIVE – SPIRIT PRAYER

Use this prayer at the start of the service, to ask God to make us sensitive to the Spirit.

> Where our lives have been so crowded with noise
> that we have drowned out the voice of your Spirit,
> Lord, have mercy.
> **Lord, have mercy.**

Where our hearts have been so overwhelmed with busyness
that we have squeezed out the presence of your Spirit,
Christ, have mercy.
Christ, have mercy.

Where we have become defensive, through stress and fear,
and we have shrugged off the touch of your Spirit,
Lord, have mercy.
Lord, have mercy.

Eternal God,
awaken our hearts to the reality of your Spirit;
invigorate our senses with the purity of your Spirit;
break down our defences with the beauty of your Spirit;
fill us afresh with the presence of your Spirit,
in the name of Christ.
Amen.

ALTERNATIVE – KITE RITUAL

Make kite shapes out of coloured cardboard. Cut lengths of string and strips of coloured plastic bags to make the tails. People tie the strips of plastic onto the string in classic kite-tail style and then attach them to the kite shapes with sticky tape. Invite people to write on the kites their need of God's Spirit; the places in their lives where they long for the Spirit of God to blow. Attach these on a string across the worship space, then lead people in prayer.

ALTERNATIVE – SPIRIT METAPHORS

Instead of the multi-sensory entrance, set up metaphors for the Spirit around the worship space that people will walk past and interact with as they enter.

- *Fire:* Use a fire wok or barbecue to have a blazing fire burning outside the church.
- *Wind:* Have a number of fans blowing in the entrance to the church. Attach to the fans ribbons that will move in the air.
- *Energy:* A plasma ball provides a fascinating metaphor for God's Spirit. You can see pulsating electrical energy; when you touch the ball, it focuses and streams toward your finger, just as God responds to us when we reach out to God.

- *Water:* Fill the font with water, if you have one in an appropriate place, or set up an indoor water feature.
- *Breath:* Have someone playing the flute, or another wind instrument, as people come in; or have mirrors that people can breathe on to see their breath.

CONNECTING WITH SCRIPTURE

- The wind blows wherever it pleases. You hear its sound, but you cannot tell where it comes from or where it is going. So it is with everyone born of the Spirit (John 3:8).
- The Spirit descended on Jesus like a dove after his baptism (Matthew 3:16).
- Jesus breathed on the disciples for them to receive the Spirit (John 20:22).
- When the Spirit came at Pentecost, there was a sound like a wind, and tongues of fire rested on the disciples (Acts 2:1–4).

HAND IT OVER

This service needs the participation of lots of young people to make it happen. Don't just tell them what to do, though. Involve them in decision-making and creativity.

Hopes and Dreams

What Happens?

People write their hopes and dreams for the future on a piece of paper and make it into a boat, which they then 'sail' on a bowl of water.

Effort Involved

Materials Needed

- Copies of the boat handout, or plain sheets of paper
- Pens
- A shallow bowl or tray of water, or some blue material to represent a river
- Instrumental music to play during the activity.

Some Thoughts

Some people in the Bible seemed to get clear instructions from God about the way their lives would turn out. Abraham was told to leave his father's house, his country and his people to become the father of God's people (Genesis 12:1–3). Mary was told that she was highly favoured and was to become the mother of God's son (Luke 1:26–38).

But other people needed to be tenacious and to take the initiative. The Canaanite woman was ignored by Jesus when she first asked him to heal her daughter. It was only when she persisted that Jesus relented (Matthew 15:21–28). Bartimaeus had to call out for attention, in spite of being told to shut up, and was then asked by Jesus to articulate what he wanted, even though it might have seemed obvious (Mark 10:46–52).

What about us? Should we sit and wait for God to tell us what to do? Or should we take steps in faith, expecting that God will show us if we are on the wrong path?

God spoke, and there were light, sky, land, plants, animals, people... Made in the image of God, we too can articulate our hopes and dreams for the future to start to call them into being. This activity gives people an opportunity to think about where they want to go with God; how they hope to see the kingdom come on earth, as it is in heaven.

How to Do it

You will need to set the context for this activity to suit your group. It may be appropriate at the start of a new year, or when people are choosing options, or leaving to go to university. Talk about your own experience of following your hopes and dreams, and of how we should understand our role in the kingdom of God. Talk about the gifts and talents that God gives us and how God expects us to use them.

Invite people to take a piece of paper and to write on it their hopes and dreams for the future. Allow some time for this, and play some appropriate music during it. If you use the handout, participants should be able to follow the instructions on the sheet to make the boat; if not, you'll need to provide instructions. In any case, have a few boats already made up, to show what they should look like.

Using appropriate words and prayers, invite people to set their boats on the water, or onto the cloth 'river', as a way of symbolizing 'setting sail' into God's purposes.

Alternative – Launch Each Other's Dreams

It can be very powerful to get people to make boats and leave them in a designated space. Later in the service, invite people to come and launch one another's dreams onto the water as they pray for the person who made that particular boat. This mirrors the help and support we often need to get started on new initiatives.

Alternative – Origami Birds

Investigate other origami shapes that might be appropriate – for example, get people to make peace cranes as a way of saying they want to give wings to their dreams.

Connecting with Scripture

- Isaiah says that once we are moving we will hear God telling us which way we should go (Isaiah 30:21).
- Jeremiah says that God knows the plans God has for us. How should we understand this verse? How much detail does God ordain for us, and how much can we shape? (Jeremiah 29:11)
- The Canaanite woman had to be persistent in her dream to see her daughter healed (Matthew 15:21–28).

Hand it Over

Encourage young people to put their names on their boats, and use the 'cloth river' idea rather than the bowl of water during the service. Gather the boats in afterwards and hold onto them for six months or so. Then hand them back to the group, either individually or as a whole. Talk about what they wrote. Have they taken steps towards their dreams? Have they changed or refined what they thought they wanted to do? Have other opportunities opened up instead? Help people to work out where they need to take the initiative, and where they need to let go of unhelpful hopes and dreams.

How to make a paper boat

 1. Fold top to bottom.

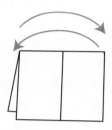 2. Fold side to side, crease and open out.

 3. Fold top corners to line up with central line.

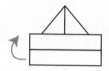 4. Fold top layer up and crease.

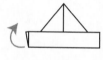 5. Turn over and do the same on the other side.

 6. Insert thumbs here and pull outward.

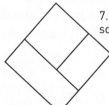 7. Flatten into a square shape.

 8. Fold top layer up to top point.

 9. Turn over and do the same on the other side.

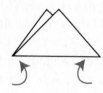 10. Insert thumbs here and pull outward.

 11. Pull outer layers down and flatten.

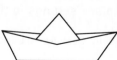 12. You now have a boat shape – voila!

Hospitality

What Happens?

People lay a table for a dinner party, to symbolize preparing a space for others to join the group.[5]

Effort Involved

Materials Needed

- A table
- Plates, cutlery, glasses, flowers, candles, salt and pepper – anything that you would use to lay a dinner table at home
- Blank place cards
- Pens
- Music to play during the activity.

Some Thoughts

I love the story of Jesus at the house of Simon the Pharisee (used as a meditation on page 99), where he is made welcome not by his respectable host, but by a woman with a bad reputation. Jesus was criticized for the people he spent time with, and he turns upside down our ideas about hospitality. It's not about being nice to our friends; it's about welcoming strangers and 'others' and making room for them.

How to Do it

Set up the empty table in an appropriate part of the room. Have the place settings piled up near it, or in boxes.

Focus on some or all of Luke 14:12–24, where Jesus tells us to invite to our homes those who won't be able to return the favour, rather than our friends and family. You could use a 'godly play' approach to get people reflecting on the parable of the great banquet, or some other way to encourage people to engage with the text.

Then invite people to consider how they can answer Jesus' call to make room for strangers and for those who are different from us. Invite people to add place settings to the table – napkins, plates, cutlery, salt,

---

5 Gwen Page, Sue Donnelly, Dean Ayres, Ben Cohen and Sarah Rundle were involved in creating this service.

pepper, candles – to symbolize wanting to create environments in which hospitality can flourish. They should pray as they do so, asking God to show them where they need to change as individuals, and where the group needs to change. Invite them to write on the place cards names of people they want to show hospitality to and to add them to the table.

Once the table is laid, invite people to reflect on its transformed appearance as a place of welcome and safety.

ALTERNATIVE – PRAYER OF WELCOME

Use this prayer to welcome people into the service. It works well to use two voices, one to read the 'This is the house of God...' sections and one to read the Bible passages.

Voice one:
This is the house of God, and whoever you are, wherever you have been, whatever you have done and whoever you know, God flings the door wide open.

Voice two:
Come, all you who are thirsty,
    come to the waters;
and you who have no money,
    come, buy and eat!
Come, buy wine and milk
    without money and without cost.
Why spend money on what is not bread,
    and your labour on what does not satisfy?
Listen, listen to me, and eat what is good,
    and you will delight in the richest of fare.

Voice one:
This is the house of God, and whatever you have done and wherever you have been, God has a place reserved for you.

Voice two:
You prepare a table before me
    in the presence of my enemies.
You anoint my head with oil;
    my cup overflows.

Voice one:
This is the house of God, and whoever you are, God invites you in.

Voice two:
Are you tired? Worn out? Burned out on religion? Come to me. Get away with me and you'll recover your life. I'll show you how to take a real rest. Walk with me and work with me – watch how I do it. Learn the unforced rhythms of grace. I won't lay anything heavy or ill-fitting on you. Keep company with me and you'll learn to live freely and lightly.

Voice one:
This is the house of God, and God is delighted to see you.

Voice two:
You're no longer wandering exiles. This kingdom of faith is now your home country. You're no longer strangers or outsiders. You belong here, with as much right to be called a follower of Christ as anyone. God is building a home. God is using us all – irrespective of how we got here – in what God is building.

Voice one:
This is the house of God, and God welcomes you here.

The Bible passages used in this prayer are: Isaiah 55:1–2; Psalm 23:5; Matthew 11:28–30 (*The Message*) and Ephesians 2:19–20 (*The Message*).

ALTERNATIVE – BARRIERS TO HOSPITALITY

Create a wall, using children's building bricks or something like Duplo – the bigger the blocks, the better. Invite people to reflect on what stops them being hospitable, and what type of people they would find it most difficult to accept – fear of other people? Being judgmental? Racism or other prejudice? Wanting to protect what they have? Invite people to remove a brick from the wall if they want that barrier removed from their lives.

Or, for a similar idea with a bigger visual impact, create a wall using empty cardboard boxes. Invite people to draw or write on the boxes their barriers to hospitality. Then, at an appropriate place in the service, break down the wall, to symbolize wanting to be open and hospitable.

Connecting with Scripture

- When Abraham welcomed strangers into his home, they gave him a message from God that would change his life (Genesis 18:1–15).
- Jesus tells us to invite to a meal those who won't be able to invite us back (Luke 14:12–24).
- Jesus was criticized for eating with 'tax collectors and sinners' (Luke 5:27–32).
- The writer of Hebrews encourages us to show hospitality to strangers, in case they are angels in disguise (Hebrews 13:2).

Hand it Over

This could be quite a challenging subject to approach with your group. Some young people are very protective of their youth group; they don't want other people coming along and spoiling it!

Collaborative Liturgy

What Happens?

People write their responses to a question during worship. These responses are then used as liturgy later in the service.

Effort Involved

● ◉ ◉

Materials Needed

Pens and paper.

Some Thoughts

I grew up in a Brethren church and was baptized in a Baptist church, both of which took pride in the freedom of their worship, unbound by dry and dusty liturgy, but both of which had patterns and rhythms of worship that were as regular as any Anglican service. I have grown to love the beauty and power of well-crafted words used in worship, especially when those words have grown out of the shared common life of a community.

The usual understanding of the word 'liturgy' is that it comes from the Greek word *leitourgia*, which means public work or duty, or the work of the people. Liturgy doesn't have to be the exclusive preserve of experts, although like any craft there is huge value in training, and in honing our gifts and abilities. This activity makes space for everyone to contribute to a part of the liturgy: for the expression of worship to truly reflect the 'work of the people'.

How to Do it

During the service, create time for people to write their responses to a question.

For example, you could tell the story from Mark 8:27–30, where Jesus asks his disciples who the crowds say he is.[6] Talk about some of the events that have led up to that question. Jesus then goes on to ask them, 'Who do you say I am?' Leave the story there, without giving Peter's response, and ask people to reflect on that question for themselves: 'Who do *you* say Jesus is?' Invite them to write down their responses.

---

6 Sue Donnelly

Gather these in and get a couple of people to read through them quickly. Then include them in some spoken liturgy along these lines:

> Jesus, you ask your disciples what the crowds are saying about you.
>   Some say you are John the Baptist; some say you are Elijah; some say you are a prophet.
>   Jesus, you ask Peter what he says about you.
>   Peter says you are the Messiah.
>   Jesus, you ask us what we say about you.
>   We say you are...
> *(And then read out the responses that people have given, one after the other)*

You probably won't have time to read all of them, but try to include as many contributions as possible. Leave out any that may be offensive, but do make space for doubts to be expressed, or for 'less than perfect' theology, as you want the prayer to be honest and authentic. This is who people say Jesus is at this point in their journeys of faith.

Another passage that can be the stimulus for this activity is Romans 8:31–39, where Paul says that nothing can separate us from the love of God. During the service invite people to reflect on the things that they feel create a distance between them and God and write these down. Then, later in the service, use them in an adaptation of this passage, pointing out that although we may feel that these things separate us from God, in reality there is nothing that can. Make this point clear. You don't want to ask people to do something and then (effectively) tell them that they're wrong to think that, by including their responses in the passage without that explanation!

You could read the passage through from verse 31 to 39, then start again at verse 35. This time instead of giving Paul's list that begins, 'trouble or hardship or...', add in seven of the things that people have written, keeping the same structure of the verse. And then, in verse 38, add in ten more, where Paul says, 'For I am convinced that neither... nor ...', again keeping the structure of the verse. You could repeat these four verses again, to include as many contributions as possible.

CONNECTING WITH SCRIPTURE

Jesus asks Peter, 'Who do you say I am?' and waits to hear his response (Mark 8:27–30).

HAND IT OVER

Give young people an opportunity to write their own versions of the liturgy that is used in your church. For example, at the beginning of the service there will be a greeting or prayer that encourages people to focus on God: to set their hearts to worshipping God. Later there will be prayers of penitence and/or a creed. Choose one of these sections and look at the structure of it with them. What do these words help us to do? Then encourage them to write their own versions, using words authentic to them. Following a structure does not have to stifle creativity; it can provide a framework in which creativity can flourish.

Confession

What Happens?

People confess their sins to God and take part in a ritual that symbolizes forgiveness.

Effort Involved

Materials Needed

- Paper, pens and a shredder
- *OR* stones, marker pens and some open water
- *OR* parsley and salt water
- *OR* helium balloons, strings, strips of card, pens, staplers, black bin bag, scissors
- *OR* sticks, nails and a fire
- *OR* mobile phones.

Some Thoughts

Confession seems to me such an important part of a worship service. We pause and ask God's spirit to bring to mind the things that we have done that have harmed our relationships with God, with others, with the planet and with ourselves. We acknowledge those before God, and ask for God's forgiveness. We receive God's forgiveness and then we choose to leave those things behind us, forgiving ourselves where necessary, making amends where necessary. And then we are free: cleansed, released, forgiven, able to start again.

But often confession is rushed, with little time to reflect or to hear from God. Often it's uniform, with everyone saying the same words and little space for personal expression. Often we are left with our sins dangling round our necks, finding it difficult to shake them off or to receive God's forgiveness.

I suspect that these ideas will be familiar, but they are included here because I think it's crucial to make space for confession and the receiving of forgiveness. Taking part in a ritual where you see the expression of your sin shredded or burned or disappeared can be a very powerful experience, which enables us to receive God's forgiveness and move on.

How to Do it

Each of these ideas need to be topped and tailed with an opportunity for reflection and a declaration of God's forgiveness. Don't miss these aspects out. When we rush into confession without stopping to think about what we need to confess, it becomes only an empty parroting of words. When we rush on to the next thing without proclaiming the forgiveness of God, we can leave people holding onto their sinfulness.

When you have given people an opportunity to confess their sins to God, always make sure that someone speaks words of forgiveness with confidence – reminding us that God has heard and has forgiven us. 1 John 1:9 and Psalm 103:11–12 are good Bible passages to use. But also refer to the ritual that has taken place, where that illustrates the way in which God deals with our sin. 'Just as your words have been destroyed in the shredder, so God deals with your sin and gives you forgiveness in its place.'

Using a Shredder

Invite people to draw, or write on pieces of paper, the things for which they need to ask for forgiveness. Then, at some point in the service, they should come forward and put them into the shredder, as a symbol of the way that God deals with our sin.

By Open Water

You can do this beside a river, canal, lake, pond, or the sea. Be aware of the risks involved in being near open water and asking people to throw stones. Check the ground near your chosen water beforehand, to see if there are enough stones around. If not, you will need to bring some with you!

Invite people to find a stone, and to find some space for quiet reflection. Invite them to hold their stone in their hand as they talk to God about the things that they want to confess. You could invite them to mark their stone with a marker pen. Then, using some suitable words, invite people to stand beside the water and throw in their stones. Can they get their stone back again? In the same way, God has wiped out our sin and offers us forgiveness in its place.

An indoor version of this could be to use sugar cubes in a bowl of warm water. When you stir the water, the cubes will dissolve.

Using Parsley and Salt Water

Invite people to take a piece of parsley, dip it into salt water and eat it. The salt water represents tears of penitence; the green herb the new life that will grow from the forgiveness that God brings.

Using Helium Balloons

Fill some balloons with helium and tie long strings to them. Invite people to write on strips of card the things that they want to confess, and to join them with other people's strips in paper chains using the stapler. Use these to weigh down the balloons. (You may like to experiment to find out how many strips of card are needed to weigh down one balloon, and instruct people accordingly.) Invite people to reflect on how the chains of sin are weighing down the balloons. Then – with suitably dramatic effect – cut the strings to let the balloons go free and gather up the chains into a plastic bin bag.

Using Sticks, Nails and Fire

This works well at a residential event, where you can have a campfire, or during worship at a barbecue. Give people a stick and a nail. Invite them to use the nail to scratch words or symbols into the stick that represent the things that they want to confess. Then invite them to throw the sticks onto the fire and watch them be burned up.

Using Mobile Phones

This will work only if everyone has access to a mobile phone. You need to set this up in advance with a text service, such as www.sms2email.co.uk. Arrange that when people send a text to a certain number beginning with the word 'confess', then they receive a message back that says 'Your sins are forgiven.' This mirrors the generous forgiveness that God offers to us, in that whatever we 'send' to God, we get the same message back that our sins are forgiven. Be aware, however, that there might be some delay in the responses coming back, so there is a potential for later parts of your service to be disrupted by bleeps from phones. Assure participants that no one will read the text messages! And be prepared to deal with people who may not have sent the text to the correct number and who don't get a message of forgiveness back; God does forgive them anyway.

CONNECTING WITH SCRIPTURE

- If we claim to be without sin, we deceive ourselves and the truth is not in us. If we confess our sins, God is faithful and just and will forgive us our sins and purify us from all unrighteousness (1 John 1:8–9).
- David talks with great confidence about God's forgiveness in Psalm 103:11–12, and writes his own heartfelt confession in Psalm 51.

Listening

What Happens?

People walk through a cloud of noise from a number of different CD or MP3 players, as a stimulus to think about listening to God and to others.[7]

Effort Involved

Materials Needed

- Recordings of six different types of sounds – see suggestions below
- CD or MP3 players on which to play them.

Some Thoughts

Listening is a skill that can be learned. It's not something that happens just because you have ears. No doubt you've been in a situation where you've been talking to someone, but you know that they're not really paying attention. Distracted by the TV, their mobile phone, or just the 'noise' inside their head, they may have heard what you said, but they haven't really listened to it.

This activity could form part of a service that leads people to reflect on how they listen to God and to each other. Think through what other aspects of listening you want to include in the service:

- Teaching or a reflection on a story from the Bible about someone who listened, such as Samuel, to God (1 Samuel 3), or Mary, to Jesus (Luke 10:38–42).
- Asking people to brainstorm what it feels like when someone really listens to you, and in contrast when they want people to listen and they don't.
- What are the obstacles that stop us listening to God and to others?

How to Do it

You will need to create recordings of six or more different types of sound. Include some that are easy to listen to – a comedy show; some music; a news bulletin; the sound of the sea – as well as some that are more difficult – a car alarm; a police siren; a baby crying; the voice of a needy

---

7 Ben Cohen helped to create this idea

person wanting attention; an argument or fight. You may be able to record some of these from the TV or radio, or find them online, or on a CD of sound effects. Others you will need to write and record especially. Involve young people as much as you can in creating these.

Set up your CD or MP3 players around the worship space. You want them spread out, so that if you stand in the centre you hear a mere cacophony of sound, but if you move closer to each player you can hear the sound it is playing. Try this out before the service and adjust the volume of the players accordingly.

When you come to use the soundscape, you will need a person at each player to turn it on when you give a signal. Explain what will happen. Invite people to move around through the noise, to try and discern each of the distinct sounds. Give time and space for this to happen. Then, on another cue, get your helpers to gradually turn the sounds down. Call people back together. Invite them to reflect on that experience. Which of the sounds were easiest to listen to? Which made you want to move on as quickly as you could? Which of the sounds demanded a response from you? Which most needed to be heard? Which sound do you think Jesus would have lingered at?

Alternative – Sound Montage

Create a sound montage, with which you can begin the service without any introduction. Start with gentle sounds of traffic and people in conversation, then add sounds that become more intrusive and complex – sirens wailing; rap bands; politicians talking. The aim is to make people feel uncomfortable. Let the sound get louder, and then stop it abruptly. The silence after it will be very sweet.

Alternative – I Am Listening To You, Honestly…

Use this during a service, to get people thinking about how good they are at listening to others. You could get different people to read the verses. Feel free to change the TV programme mentioned to one that you watch, and the references to 'work' to relate to 'school', if that's more appropriate.

> I am listening to you, honestly,
> But I'm also thinking about what I'm going to say next.
> I hate embarrassed gaps in conversation when no one knows what to say.
> I want you to think that I'm interesting, funny, witty,
> So I'm lining up my response, getting it ready.

I am listening to you, honestly,
But I hope you don't go on too long;
I want to catch the final scores, to find out how my team has done,
And I need to ring my friend before he goes out for the evening.
Then Desperate Housewives *is on TV, and I don't want to miss that;*
So make it quick, and you don't need to repeat yourself.

I am listening to you, honestly,
But I'm also thinking about what happened at work this week –
And what I've got to do next week –
I'm going to be in trouble if I don't get that report written,
And I need to work out why my colleague isn't talking to me,
So it's quite hard to hear what you're saying
Over all this internal noise.

I am listening to you, honestly,
But that group over there looks like they're having a much better
conversation;
They're laughing and joking.
I'd really like to get to know some of them –
Not that you're not important – of course you are;
I just wish I had the chance to speak to them, too.

I am listening to you, honestly,
But to be honest, I really wish you'd listen to me –
Just for once – to pay attention to what I have to say,
Without jumping in with your experience and your solutions.
I don't want you to solve my problems;
I just want you to hear me:
To hear the 'me' behind the words;
To really listen.

ALTERNATIVE – ANOINTING EARLOBES

As a responsive ritual, invite people to have their earlobes anointed with oil, as a sign that they want to be better listeners, to God and to others, in the future. Provide some scented oil and have a couple of members of your team anoint people and speak words of blessing over them.

Connecting with Scripture

- At the end of the parable of the sower, Jesus said, 'Whoever has ears to hear, let them hear' (Mark 4:9). It's a phrase he used at other times, and which is repeated in the letters to the churches in Revelation (Revelation 2 and 3). It implies that listening is a choice that we need to make, rather than something that happens automatically.
- Samuel hears God calling his name, although he doesn't recognize who it is. It takes Eli a while to realize that it is God who is speaking to this boy. What do young people hear from God that we don't have ears to hear? (1 Samuel 3)

Hand it Over

Involve young people in creating the sounds for the soundscape. Get them to choose which sounds to include and then to record and edit them. Many of them will have access to appropriate software, at home or at school, and for some it will fit with music technology, media, or art courses.

Encourage young people to consider how good they are at listening to each other. Do they tend to be distracted by MP3 players, mobile phones and the like?

Labels

What Happens?

People think about the labels that they 'wear', from what others have said about them and what they say about themselves. They swap these labels for one that God gives them.

Effort Involved

Materials Needed

- Lots of cardboard luggage labels: at least three for each person. If you can get three different colours, so much the better.
- Four large mirror tiles or old mirrors
- Four large sheets of card or flipchart paper
- Marker pens: the type used to write on CDs
- Felt pens
- Two large bowls or containers for the label exchange: one to hold the labels with God's words on, and one where people can discard their negative labels
- Music to play during the activity.

Some Thoughts

Words are powerful. Words of encouragement and affirmation can strengthen and inspire us. We can grow to fill aspirational words that describe our potential. Speaking words of blessing over people's lives can help to call into being embryonic qualities.

But we can also carry around with us hurtful things that people said to us a long time after they have forgotten the incident. We can wear 'labels' that we have given ourselves at some point in our lives, but we forget to examine whether they still fit us, and we keep wearing them long after they have passed their 'sell by' date.

This activity encourages people to name the positive and negative labels that they 'wear' and gives them the opportunity to swap the negative labels for words that God says about us. Think through whether this activity is suitable for your group; it can raise quite strong feelings, so make sure that the group members will be able to benefit from the activity.

How to Do it

You will need to create four similar areas. Each should have a large mirror tile or old mirror attached securely to the wall. Write one of the following headings on each of the pieces of card and attach it next to one of the mirrors:

- Positive things others say about me
- Positive things I say about myself
- Negative things others say about me
- Negative things I say about myself.

By each mirror place a couple of pens that people can use to write on it. You will also need a pile of felt pens and some blank luggage labels. If you are able to get hold of three different colours of luggage labels, use one colour for the positive areas, one for the negative areas and one for the words that God says about us. If not, then write the word POSITIVE on some labels and NEGATIVE on others and place them at the appropriate stations. Each person needs to have one positive label, one negative label and one with God's words on it.

Make these areas aesthetically pleasing. You could use Christmas-tree lights around the mirrors.

Prepare the set of labels with words from the Bible on. Cut out the words from the following pages and stick each one on a luggage label; or, preferably, write them by hand – see the suggestion in 'Hand it Over' below. Put these luggage labels in a bowl or similar container and create a fifth area in your worship space, where people will exchange their negative label for the words that God says about them.

You may want to create written instructions by each of the mirrors that explain what people need to do. You'll need to write something like this for each one – adapt these words as appropriate for the other stations:

> *What are the positive words that people have said about you during your life – words of encouragement; words that make you feel great?*
> *Write them on the mirror and on your positive/blue label.*

Introduce the activity during the worship service. Talk about your own experience of positive or negative labels that you received when you were younger – positive things that others said to you and that you said about yourself as well as negative labels. Talk about the power that these can have to define who we are, both positively and negatively. Talk about the importance of discarding labels that are not true, or no longer true, and of hearing what God says about us.

Invite people to take some time visiting the four stations and writing on the mirrors and on their labels the positive and negative things that they and others have said about themselves. You could lead the way, writing one word yourself on each of the four mirrors and on your labels, to show people what to do. Explain that when the mirrors are full people should write on the sheets of card instead.

Play some appropriate music and give people time and space to interact with the four areas. You may want to ask some of your team to watch out for those who may find doing so difficult.

Once everyone has had a chance to visit the four stations, invite people to sit down and reflect on the activity. Talk about the impact – both positive and negative – of looking at the mirrors with the words on them. You could lead people in prayer, asking God to heal people of any hurt that has been caused through the negative labels, and asking God to help them own and grow into the positive ones.

Then invite people to come and swap their negative label for one that contains words that God says about them. Play some music and allow time and space for this to happen.

Make sure that people know who they can talk to if this activity has raised issues for them, and be prepared to follow the activity up in conversation and in further sessions, as appropriate.

Connecting with Scripture

- When Jesus first met Simon, he gave him a new name – Peter, the rock on which he would build his church (John 1:42).
- Hosea called his daughter Lo-Ruhamah, which means 'not loved', and his son Lo-Ammi', which means 'not my people', to mirror how God felt about the people of Israel. Poor children – I wonder how that affected their lives? (Hosea 1:6–9)

Hand it Over

Invite young people to help you write by hand the labels that give God's perspective. It takes time, but provides a far more personal experience that will have a big impact on the people who receive them. Make the word in capitals stand out; this is the one-word summary of the verse. But do make sure that you include the whole verse and Bible reference, so that people can look them up later.

And as you write, you can be praying for the person who will pick up that label: that he or she will be able to accept this truth and make it a part of their life. You can also pray for yourself: that you too will be able to live in the truth of these words.

CREATED
God created my inmost being; God knit me together in my mother's womb.
Psalm 139:13

WONDERFUL
I am fearfully and wonderfully made.
Psalm 139:14

CHOSEN
God chose me... before the creation of the world to be holy and blameless in God's sight.
Ephesians 1:4

BLESSED
God has blessed me... with every spiritual blessing in Christ.
Ephesians 1:3

LOVED
Because of God's great love for me, God, who is rich in mercy, made me alive in Christ.
Ephesians 2:4

CREATED
I am God's handiwork, created in Christ Jesus to do good works.
Ephesians 2:10

LOVED
Christ loved me and gave himself up for me as a fragrant offering... to God.
Ephesians 5:2

CALLED
God says: 'I have summoned you by name; you are mine.'
Isaiah 43:1

PROTECTED
When you pass through the waters, I will be with you... When you walk through the fire, you will not be burned.
Isaiah 43:2

HONOURED

God says: 'You are precious and honoured in my sight, and... I love you.'
Isaiah 43:4

FORGIVEN

God forgives all your sins and heals all your diseases.
Psalm 103:3

REDEEMED

God redeems your life... and crowns you with love and compassion.
Psalm 103:4

LOVED

From everlasting to everlasting, the Lord's love is with you who fear him.
Psalm 103:17

FAVOURED

The Lord God is your sun and shield; the Lord bestows favour and honour on you.
Psalm 84:11

PROTECTED

God is your refuge and strength, an ever-present help in trouble.
Psalm 46:1

ACCOMPANIED

The Lord Almighty is with you; the God of Jacob is your fortress.
Psalm 46:7

CHERISHED

God says: 'I will not forget you! See, I have engraved you on the palms of my hands.'
Isaiah 49:15–16

PROTECTED

God will instruct you and teach you in the way you should go; God will counsel you with God's loving eye on you.
Psalm 32:8

STRENGTHENED
God gives strength to the weary and increases the power of the weak. Hope in the Lord; God will renew your strength.
Isaiah 40:29, 31

CHOSEN
You are a chosen people, a holy nation, God's special possession.
1 Peter 2:9

PROTECTED
You are the apple of God's eye. God keep you in the shadow of God's wings.
Psalm 17:8

SIGNIFICANT
You are the salt of the earth... You are the light of the world.
Matthew 5:13, 14

HOLY
You are holy in God's sight, without blemish and free from accusation.
Colossians 1:22

CHAMPIONED
God is for you, who can be against you?
Romans 8:31

PRECIOUS
Nothing can separate you from the love of Christ.
Romans 8:31–39

LOVED
You are God's child... born of God.
John 1:12, 13

VALUABLE
God knows how many hairs there are on your head; you are valuable to God.
Luke 12:7

PROTECTED
The Lord is your light and salvation... The Lord is the stronghold of your life.
Psalm 27:1

Do it Yourself

What Happens?

People use a selection of words – a sense, an object, a fruit of the Spirit – as a stimulus to create worship stations.

Effort Involved

Materials Needed

- Copies of the photocopiable sheets, or your own versions
- Bowls or containers
- At a later time, you will need further materials to actually create the stations.

Some Thoughts

The biggest block to creativity is telling yourself that you are not creative.[8] Made in the image of a creative God, we all have the ability to create, invent, discover, express and explore. But there are ways in which you can encourage creativity, and ways in which it can be stifled. Hand someone a completely blank sheet of paper and tell them to 'be creative', and you'll find their minds will often go as blank as the paper. Provide people with a task and some constraints within which they have to achieve it, and their creative juices will start to flow.

The photocopiable sheets give some constraints for this exercise to create worship stations – a sense, an object and a fruit of the Spirit – but feel free to choose your own constraints to fit in with the theme of the service, or with matters you have been studying with the youth group recently.

A 'station' is a creative space for people to visit and interact with during a worship service. It provides a focus for worship or prayer. It helps if it's visually stimulating, with words, images, or film to watch. It can include verses from the Bible to read; questions to reflect on; a ritual to take part in; or some way of responding to the material that's there.

It's best to do this with a group who have had some experience of creative worship, so that they have a fund of ideas and experiences to

---

8   See *A Whack on the Side of the Head: How you can be more creative*, by Roger von Oech (Wellingborough: Thorsons, 3rd edn 1990).

draw on. This activity involves them in planning for a future service, but encourages them to see the planning as part of their worship.

How to Do it

Cut up the photocopiable sheets into cards, fold them and put each type into a separate bowl, so that people can easily pick out a sense, an object and a fruit of the Spirit. If you have decided to use different constraints, you will need to make your own sheets.

Talk to the group about worship stations, asking them what they have found helpful and what things they think work best. Talk about the theme you have chosen for the service, or include them in choosing the theme. You may want to do some Bible study with the group, to make sure that they have a solid foundation from which to work.

Get people into small groups of two or three. Invite them to pick one card from each bowl. Then invite them to create a worship station, using those words as stimuli. The aim of each station is to help people reflect on and engage with that fruit of the Spirit. Invite them to think about what people will see at their station; what they will read; what they will do. Encourage them to be as creative as possible.

Then leave them to it. Be around to answer questions, if they have any. Once the stations have been planned, you will need to help the group members to access resources to create the stations for the service. You'll also need to plan how the service will begin and end, and any other aspects that you may want to include in it.

Connecting with Scripture

- Jesus sent the disciples out on their own to put into practice what they had seen him do. They went out with few resources, like sheep among wolves. Would we have been that trusting, or would we have wanted more control? (Matthew 10:1–42)
- The fruit of the Spirit is love, joy, peace, patience, kindness, goodness, faithfulness, gentleness, self-control (Galatians 5:22–23).

Hand it Over

That's what you're doing with this activity – handing it over to members of your group. Sit on your hands and don't interfere; although you can be ready to answer questions, if they ask them. Let them learn by doing: by making mistakes and taking risks.

taste	taste
touch	touch
smell	smell
hearing	hearing
sight	sight

playdough	feather
stone	chocolate
candle	grapes
paper	balloon
ice cube	map of local area

cloth	piece of string
love	love
joy	joy
peace	peace
patience	patience

kindness	kindness
goodness	goodness
faithfulness	faithfulness
gentleness	gentleness
self-control	self-control

CHAPTER 3

The Bible

The Bible is more than a collection of stories, laws, sayings and history. It is the record of God's dealings with humanity, from the beginning of time to the present day. In its pages we encounter God, and we find ourselves, as we read how God intervened in the lives of people like us, and the ways in which they responded. We discover timeless wisdom that helps us to live in cultures and contexts very different from the ones in which the Bible's words were originally written.

These activities create opportunities for people to respond to texts from the Bible in worship and prayer. They encourage people to engage with the text creatively, exploring what it says and how it might apply to their own lives.

One thing we need to be aware of as we approach the Bible is how it has been used and abused in the past to control people's lives and to perpetuate injustice. Another is the fact that parts of it are understood and interpreted in very different ways by people who are all genuinely seeking to follow Christ. Youth workers have a huge responsibility as they teach young people to understand and apply the words of the Bible. You need to teach the Christian faith while also encouraging young people to think and to hear from God for themselves. You need to resist the temptation to control and dictate, but trust the Spirit of God to lead them into all truth.

Miracles Liturgy

WHAT HAPPENS?

This creates a space for people to be honest about their doubts, while also expressing their faith in God.

EFFORT INVOLVED

MATERIALS NEEDED

- Words on the accompanying sheet
- An OHP or data projector, if you want to project the response for people to join in
- Paper
- Pens.

SOME THOUGHTS

Planning a worship service on the theme of miracles was challenging. On the one hand, we had the stories from Scripture of Jesus healing people and testimonies from people's lives about God intervening in miraculous ways. On the other hand, many people in our community seemed desperately in need of miracles, yet God was silent and still. How could we be true to both realities?

The story of Shadrach, Meshach and Abednego provided inspiration. Faced with being thrown into the fiery furnace, they stated honestly their belief in God: that if God were able to deliver them, they would be saved, but even if God didn't, God was still God. The liturgy on the photocopiable page was written to help us express that tension – believing that God could act, but that, whatever happened, God was still God. Somehow, the honesty of the piece proved more powerful than simple statements of faith that left no room for the reality that we faced.

There isn't much of a technique to pass on in this activity; simply a plea for honesty, and for space to allow doubts to be expressed alongside faith. Feel free to adapt and use the miracles liturgy, if doing so suits your own situation.

How to Do it

The Psalms are honest expressions of doubt and faith; of joy and pain; of certainty and abandonment. You could use a reading of Psalm 13 as a stimulus for people to write about the place they themselves are in. This may work better with a small group who are preparing something that will be used later in a service. David is honest about his feelings. He feels forgotten by God, weighed down by sorrow and close to death. But he ends with a decision to trust in God, to remind himself of what God has done in the past.

Guide people to write each 'half' of their own psalms separately. First, encourage them to write honestly about any feelings of doubt and despair.

Then give them space to call to mind the things that God has done for them in the past. On another piece of paper, encourage them to write down statements of faith in God. This will be easier for them to do if they are not writing immediately next to the feelings of doubt and pain.

Read Psalm 13 again, pointing out that David holds together both doubt and faith. Encourage people to put their separate statements together and to read out their own psalms of honesty.

It may also be important to talk about the 'We believe...' statements that are part of a creed said in church. By saying, 'We believe...', we are affirming that this is the faith of the wider body of Christ of which we are a part; that this is the faith of the church that we belong to; and that we aspire to own these statements fully for ourselves, even if we struggle with some of them.

Connecting with Scripture

- In Psalm 13, David expresses his despair and feelings of alienation from God, but still ends with a declaration of faith in God.
- Shadrach, Meshach and Abednego express their faith in who God is, even though they are not sure how God will act (Daniel 3:16–18).
- Jesus challenges a father who wants his son to be healed about whether he believes it is possible. The man replies, 'I do believe; help me overcome my unbelief!' (Mark 9:14–29)

Lord God,
You spoke into darkness and chaos and then there was light;
You imagined this earth in its complexity and beauty and called it into
      being;
You created humanity in your own image and gave us a home to live in;
We believe you can do miracles.
But even if you don't, you are still God.

Lord God,
You walked with Shadrach, Meshach and Abednego through the fiery
      furnace;
You shut the mouths of hungry lions and kept Daniel safe until morning;
You gave Hannah a family when she despaired of ever having a child;
We believe you can do miracles.
But even if you don't, you are still God.

Lord God,
You changed water into wine so the wedding party could continue;
You calmed a storm, and your disciples, with words of quiet authority;
You transformed a boy's picnic into a meal for a multitude, with plenty
      left over;
We believe you can do miracles.
But even if you don't, you are still God.

Lord God,
You healed a woman from 12 years of bleeding and rejection;
You asked Bartimaeus what he wanted and then restored his sight;
You watched a paralysed man being lowered through the roof and helped
      him to his feet;
We believe you can do miracles.
But even if you don't, you are still God.

Lord God,
You called Lazarus from the tomb and restored him to life;
You walked past the mourners at Jairus' house and gave his daughter
      back to him;
You suffered a horrendous crucifixion and defeated sin and death;
We believe you can do miracles.
But even if you don't, you are still God.

Lord God,
You told your disciples that they would do greater things than you had
    done;
We hear and read stories of miracles in our world – of you healing the
    sick, setting prisoners free, releasing drug addicts from their
    addiction;
Providing the right amount of money at just the right time;
We believe you can do miracles.
But even if you don't, you are still God.

And yet, Lord, we don't see many miracles happening around us:
We have friends with cancer, and we pray, and they are not healed;
We have friends who long for children, and we pray, and they do not
    conceive.
Our doubt is mixed with faith;
Our trust is accompanied by questions.
We acknowledge the mystery of faith and prayer, and the ways in which
    they are connected;
We acknowledge that you often do things differently from the way we
    would do them;
We long to know you better, to understand more of your ways,
And we believe you can do miracles.
But even if you don't, you are still God.

Lord, we believe.
Help our unbelief.

Meditation

What Happens?

People meditate on the story of the woman anointing Jesus' feet with perfume, entering into the narrative and encountering God for themselves.

Effort Involved

Materials Needed

- Cushions
- A low table
- Crockery and cutlery to set the table for dinner
- Glasses, candles and flowers
- Perfume and a small bowl to pour it into
- Bread and grape juice, enough for everyone to have a small amount each
- Instrumental music to play softly in the background.

Some Thoughts

The psalmist talks about someone whose 'delight is in the law of the Lord, and who meditates on it day and night' and calls this person blessed. Christians throughout history have proved these words true as they have meditated prayerfully on the Bible, found hidden gems of insight and been transformed by the experience.

Christian meditation is not about emptying our minds, but about filling them with the riches of Scripture, entering into the stories and experiences and allowing God to challenge and change us through encountering him. It is an experience of listening with our ears to the word of God while we also listen with our hearts to what God is saying to us.

This is a retelling of Jesus eating dinner at the house of Simon the Pharisee, where the woman anointed his feet with perfume (Luke 7:36–50). People are invited to pray as they listen to the story and to use their imaginations to picture what it would have been like to be there as one of the guests. They will be asked to think about how they respond to the story and who they identify with. Are they people who love much because they have been forgiven much? They are invited to eat bread and drink the grape juice, to show that they too want to experience the forgiveness of Jesus.

How to Do it

Take some time to create the right visual context for this story. Set up a low table as if people were coming round to dinner – with plates, candles, glasses and flowers. The table needs to be low so that people can sit around it and see it. Arrange the lighting so that the table is clearly lit and the edges of the room are darker. Have some bread and a bottle of grape juice in the centre of the table. Put cushions around the table, so that people can move them and choose where they will sit. Think about how people will use each of their senses – if there is a kitchen nearby, you could have some bread baking so there is an inviting smell, for example.

Choose some instrumental music to play softly in the background. This will help people relax and will cover up any fidgeting or coughing.

The words that the leader reads are on the accompanying photocopiable page. You will need to leave appropriate pauses for people to think and pray. Suggestions are given for when to pause, but read the words through several times in advance to get a feel for how you will lead it.

Start the meditation outside the room where it will take place. Say the words at the beginning of the meditation and then pray. Then invite people to enter the room and take part as you guide them.

When the perfume is mentioned in the story, pour out a few drops on the table to allow people to experience the scent.

At the end, tell people that they are welcome to stay in the room and pray for as long as they like, or they are free to go. After a suitable pause, leave the room, to show that the formal meditation is over. Be available outside to talk to people about the experience.

Connecting with Scripture

- God tells Joshua to meditate on the Book of the Law and to be careful to do everything written in it (Joshua 1:8).
- The person who delights in God's word and meditates on it day and night is blessed, according to the psalmist (Psalm 1:1–3).

Hand it Over

When they have experienced this activity, you could ask the young people to prepare a similar text on a different encounter that someone had with Jesus. Encourage them to think about how they can get people to use their senses in the retelling of the story. Work with them to refine their words, and then get them to lead the group in a meditation.

Words to say outside the room

You are invited to dinner with Jesus. I am going to tell you a story, an event that happened in Jesus' life. Use your imagination to think what it would be like to be watching it happen. I will read the story to you and ask questions to prompt your thinking. I'll leave lots of space for you to pray and meet with God. Let's make this whole experience a prayer and ask that we will hear what God wants to say to us.

Prayer

Father God, we thank you for the riches of Scripture, and especially the stories of Jesus' life. We commit this time of prayer to you. Anoint our imaginations with your Spirit and speak to us. Show us how we can be transformed by this encounter, in Jesus name. Amen.

Invitation to enter the room

Jesus has been invited to dinner at the house of Simon the Pharisee. Imagine that you are one of the other guests, arriving to have dinner; perhaps curious about this teacher, who seems to have such a large following. Will you come in, and sit down around the table?
(Lead the group into the room.)

Imagine that Jesus is sitting here (indicate a place next to the table). Where will you sit? Close to him? Or at a distance, so you can watch without getting involved? Choose your place and make yourself comfortable.
(Allow people to get settled.)
Use your imagination – what can you see? What can you smell? What can you hear?
(Pause)

When one of the Pharisees invited Jesus to have dinner with him, Jesus went to the Pharisee's house and reclined at the table.
Why did Simon invite Jesus?
What is the atmosphere like – relaxed? Full of unspoken expectation?
Picture the guests gathering. Who do they greet? How do they relate to Jesus?
(Pause)

A woman in that town who lived a sinful life learned that Jesus was eating at the Pharisee's house, so she came there with an alabaster jar of perfume.
What's your reaction when this sinful woman turns up? Does she belong here? How are the other guests responding? (Pause)

As she stood behind him at his feet, weeping, she began to wet his feet with her tears. Then she wiped them with her hair, kissed them and poured perfume on them.
(Pour out some of the perfume into a small bowl.)
Would you dare to be that intimate with Jesus? How do you think Jesus feels? What do the other guests do? (Pause)

When the Pharisee who had invited him saw this, he said to himself: 'If this man were a prophet, he would know who is touching him and what kind of woman she is – that she is a sinner.'
How do you know what Simon is thinking? What does he do? How does he look? What do you think of the woman and what she has done? (Pause)

Jesus answered him, 'Simon I have something to tell you.'
'Tell me, teacher,' he said.
'Two men owed money to a certain moneylender. One owed 500 denarii and the other 50. Neither of them had the money to pay him back, so he forgave the debts of both. Now, which of them will love him more?'
What is Simon thinking? What does he do? What would you say if Jesus asked you the question? (Pause)

Simon replied, 'I suppose the one who had the bigger debt forgiven.'
'You have judged correctly,' Jesus said. Then he turned towards the woman...
What does the woman see in Jesus' eyes? Where does Simon look – at the woman, or at Jesus, or at the floor? Where do you look? (Pause)

... he turned towards the woman and said to Simon, 'Do you see this woman?'
What does Jesus mean? Of course Simon has seen the woman – he called her a sinner. What does Jesus mean? (Pause)

Jesus turned towards the woman and said to Simon, 'Do you see this woman? I came into your house. You did not give me any water for my feet, but she wet my feet with her tears and wiped them with her hair. You did not give me a kiss, but this woman, from the time I entered, has not stopped kissing my feet. You did not put oil on my head, but she has poured perfume on my feet.'
How have you welcomed Jesus when he has come to meet you? Like Simon, or like the woman? Why? (Pause)

'Therefore, I tell you, her many sins have been forgiven – as her great love has shown. But whoever who has been forgiven little loves little.' Then Jesus said to her, 'Your sins are forgiven.'

HEART, SOUL, MIND, STRENGTH (PHOTOCOPIABLE SHEET)

How much have you been forgiven? How much forgiveness have you received? What does Jesus say to you? (Pause)

The other guests began to say among themselves, 'Who is this, who even forgives sins?' Jesus said to the woman, 'Your faith has saved you; go in peace.' (Pause)

Do you want to receive forgiveness from Jesus? Stay here and eat some bread and drink some grape juice. Enjoy being with Jesus. You can stay here as long as you like; until you are ready to go in peace.

Stained-Glass Windows

What Happens?

Use your church architecture as a stimulus for engaging with the Bible in prayer and worship.

Effort Involved

Materials Needed

These will depend on your own church building and the thoughts it inspires.

Some Thoughts

Where the pillars meet the balcony in our church, there are sculptures of the heads of the Minor Prophets. They all look remarkably the same – men with flowing locks and beards – but fortunately have their names carved on scrolls, so we know who they are. For one service, we set up a station underneath each of the heads, encouraging people to engage with the themes of the relevant Bible book and to read some of its text.

For example, under Haggai we set up a cardboard shelter with a blanket for a bed and an adaptation of words from Haggai 1:3 written on its walls: 'Is this a time for you yourselves to be living in your panelled houses, when my people are living in desperate poverty around the world?' People could take away with them a 'Make Poverty History' band as a commitment to fighting poverty, as that campaign was taking place that year. Under Joel was a CD of words and music to listen to, inspired by Joel 2:28, and a mirror to look into as you reflected on your own dreams and visions.[9]

The service got us reading and studying passages of the Bible that we would rarely normally read. It also made us look at the church building in a different way, noticing aspects that we had previously missed, and thus having a visual reminder in the following months of the service that we had participated in and the things we felt God had said to us.

If your church is newly built, or if you meet in a school or other building, you may find visual stimuli like these difficult to discover. Perhaps the challenge for you is to create works of art that point people towards God, or that encourage them to engage with passages from the Bible.

---

9   Joel Baker and Simon Burrell

How to Do it

You obviously need to look round your church and see what aspects of the architecture you can use as a stimulus for praise and worship. But many churches have stained-glass windows that express biblical stories, so that's what I'll talk about here. In the days when few members of the congregation could read, these windows would effectively have been their Bible, helping them to understand and remember key stories.

This kind of worship lends itself well to stations – areas set up under each window that have words and materials to provide a specific focus for worship and prayer. You can start and end the worship with everyone gathered together, but then during it allow time for people to walk round and engage with the stations as they want to.

Each station could have a Bible text to read, a space for people to sit and look at the window, and an opportunity for a response. Provide clear written instructions, so that people know what to do. Here are some ideas based on the stories depicted in windows in my own church.

Jesus as Living Bread

Have John 6:43–51 for people to read, either in Bibles or printed out from a website such as www.biblegateway.com. Provide some freshly baked bread for people to eat. Invite people to reflect as they eat on how their relationship with Jesus sustains them. Do they take time to feed on his words regularly? Are they feeding on the right things to keep them spiritually healthy?

Christ Saves Peter from Drowning

Have Matthew 14:22–33 for people to read. Get someone to write an imaginative retelling of the story from Peter's perspective – his reflections from after the event – inspired by the image in the window. Record this on CD or MP3 and have it available for people to listen to. Have a toy boat at the station. Invite people to write on paper the doubts that 'keep them in the boat' instead of following where Jesus calls them. They can fold these up and leave them in the toy boat, as a way of saying that they want to respond to Jesus' call.

The Beatitudes

Have some magazines available, as a reminder of the messages that we get from our culture. Get people to begin by reflecting on what our culture tells us that we need to be happy. Have some strips of paper with the words, 'You'll be happy if you...' written on them twice. Invite people to finish the first sentence according to what the culture says. Then get them to read Matthew 5:3–12 and then to rewrite one of the Beatitudes in their own words on the same slip of paper, finishing the second sentence. Invite people to reflect on the juxtaposition of the words. Which of these is easiest to live by? Which of these is worth living by? Which is true? Invite them to tear the strip in two and take with them the statement that they want to live by.

If there are enough windows to have a choice, pick ones that provide a coherent theme for the service – such as people's encounters with Jesus, or Old Testament characters who met God.

CONNECTING WITH SCRIPTURE

The tabernacle that God told the Israelites to build was rich in symbolism and in visual stimuli to worship (Exodus 25–30), as was the temple that Solomon built (1 Kings 5–7). Perhaps the part that we are most familiar with is the curtain separating off the Holy of Holies, which was torn in two when Jesus died on the cross (Matthew 27:51).

HAND IT OVER

This is an ideal activity in which to engage young people. Get them to explore the church with you. Find out which aspects of the architecture they understand, and which don't mean anything. Get them to read the stories represented in the windows, and in other aspects of the church building, and then help you to set up stations that encourage people to engage with these stories.

Parable of the Sower

What Happens?

People listen to the parable of the sower and draw a picture of themselves as a plant, to represent their spiritual growth.

Effort Involved

● ● ●

Materials Needed

- Paper and pens (you could do this on one big sheet with everyone gathered round, or hand out separate sheets of paper)
- Music to play during the activity.

Some Thoughts

One response to a story is to ask yourself where you are in it. Which character do you most identify with? Which character would you most like to be? Many of Jesus' parables invite us to do that. But sometimes it can be hard to put into words what is going on in our heads, hearts and lives, so we may need to use a different tactic to uncover what's going on.

How to Do it

Make sure everyone has access to paper and a pen and enough space to draw comfortably.

Tell the story of the sower. It's very short, so you may want simply to read it a couple of times from a Bible. Or use the text on the next page, which is a more imaginative retelling that invites people to enter into the story.

Invite people to imagine their relationship with God as a plant (text for this is included at the end of the next page) and to draw it on the paper in front of them. Play some music while they do this, and encourage them to take their time.

Make sure there are opportunities for people to talk and pray about their pictures. Once the drawings are finished, you could get people to talk in twos or threes, explaining their pictures to one another and then praying for one another. Or get small groups to do that with one of the leaders. Or, if you have only a few members in your group, do it all together. Encourage people to think about how they can overcome obstacles to their growth. Which do they need to do something about? Which need God's intervention? Which do they need help with?

Connecting with Scripture

Accounts of Jesus telling the story of the sower are in Matthew 13:1–8, Mark 4:1–8 and Luke 8:1–8.

Hand it Over

This is an exercise that people can come back to every so often, to see how they have changed and grown since the last time they did it. It could be a useful tool to use with people whom you mentor.

The Parable of the Sower

You are sitting on a bench at the edge of a field. The sun is out and you can feel its warmth on your back. It's rained recently, and you can smell the green of the trees and the freshly dug earth in the field. Birds are singing in the trees next to you. You take a deep breath and enjoy the stillness of this place.

And then you see a farmer walking across the field with a bag of seed, the strap across his body. Every so often he dips his hand into the bag and pulls out a handful of seed, which he scatters on the ground in one sweeping motion. You imagine what it must be like to be that farmer: sowing crops in the hope that they will grow; needing a good harvest to make your living. The movements of his arm mark out a regular rhythm, punctuated by the patter of the seed as it falls on the ground.

You watch where the seed falls, and you imagine what will happen to it. Some seed falls on the path, where the ground is hard and impenetrable. It bounces as it lands. Already the birds are landing to eat it up. That seed is not going to produce anything at all.

Some seed falls on rocky places, where the earth is shallow. You imagine it springing up in the next few days: hopeful shoots raising their heads to the sun. But the sun is too strong for them, and their roots can't sustain them. These plants wither and die.

Some seed falls among thistles and thorns. You imagine it trying its best to grow, but it is choked by the weeds and crowded out by the thistles. With no space to flourish, it gives up and shrinks back to the earth.

But some seed falls on good soil: soil that has been dug, soil that has been weeded, soil that has been fertilized; rich soil that is a great home for a tiny seed. You imagine it putting down roots, sending up shoots, stretching towards the sun, soaking up the rain, and growing into a strong healthy plant that produces 30, 60 or even 100 seeds.

Jesus told this story many years ago. He said the seed is like the word of God. The path is like people who don't understand God's word; it gets snatched away before it has a chance to take root.

The rocky ground is like people who hear God's word and think it's great, but that enthusiasm doesn't last very long. They don't put down roots, so when trouble comes they just give up.

The thorns and thistles are like the worries and cares of this world. Some people begin to grow, but then money pressures or worries about work choke them and they never grow strong.

But some people are like the good soil. They hear God's word and make sure they understand it. They do what it says and grow strong and tall, producing lots of seed.

What about you? Imagine your relationship with God as a plant, growing in soil. How strong is the plant? How much has it grown?

What does it feed on? Is there anything stopping its growth? Or getting in the way?

Take some time to draw that plant. Ask God to help you draw what's really going on.

Elijah and the Still Small Voice

WHAT HAPPENS?

The structure of the service follows the events of a Bible story, to help people engage with the narrative.[10]

EFFORT INVOLVED

MATERIALS NEEDED

- An exercise bicycle on a turbo trainer, or a running treadmill
- Ability to project words and images onto screens
- Various film clips, sourced and created (details below)
- Music to fit the different sections of the service
- Food and drink, in a café area
- Cardboard boxes, to create an earthquake
- A candle and matches

SOME THOUGHTS

This is an experiential approach to studying the Bible, taking people through the events of a story in sequence and helping them to experience for themselves some of what was going on. This example is of Elijah running for his life and then encountering God on Mount Horeb, but you can of course use the same approach to other Bible passages. What you need to do is to identify the 'bones' of the story – what are the key events that take place? Then you'll need to consider how you can help people to experience or reflect on those.

HOW TO DO IT

These were the sections of the story that we picked up on, explained through the structure of the service. You'll be able to work out how to set them up from this description. Think carefully about the use of the worship space – where will people sit? How can you help them to feel secure enough, so that they enter into the worship, but also open to new things? How will they move around? How will they know where to go next?

---

10 Kathy Baxter, Adam Baxter and Jonny Baker

"Elijah was Afraid and Ran for his Life"

Just before the start of the service, get someone to ride on a bike on a turbo trainer, or run on a treadmill, in the centre of the worship space. You'll need someone who can keep going for ten minutes or more and who can look as if they are 'running for their life'. They should wear sunglasses, so that they don't have to make eye contact with any of the participants in the service.

Some questions are projected on screens – When do you run? What causes you to panic? What do you run from?

As people arrive, invite them to sit in the worship space and reflect on the questions. You may want to provide printed sheets that explain what people should do.

Choose some music to fit the action – a driving beat, with a sense of urgency.

"I Have Had Enough; Take My Life"

On a prearranged cue, the person running/cycling stops and collapses dramatically on the floor. The music changes mood. Someone should read or tell the story in 1 Kings 19:1–5a, where Elijah fell asleep under the tree. If you can get hold of film clips of athletes collapsing, show those on the screens at this point.

Get people to discuss in small groups: have you ever felt exhausted, like Elijah? Where was God? Have you ever 'just given up' – or wanted to give up? Have you ever collapsed after running? Is it time you did?

"Get Up and Eat"

Tell the next part of the story (verses 5b–9a). Elijah's quest seemed spiritual – to find God in his despair – but his need was physical – to eat, drink and rest. Is there really such a distinction between the two? Can we separate out body, mind and spirit, or does what happens to one happen to all? How good are we at looking after our bodies? What impact does that have on our minds and spirits?

Invite people to move to a different part of the worship space, or even into another room, where there is a café-style set-up, with tables, chairs, food and drink. Have signs on the wall that say 'Relax', 'Eat and drink', or other appropriate phrases. This may feel different from what we normally associate with worship, but that's the point! Choose appropriate music to create a sense of relaxation and to give people space to engage with the activity.

"I Am the Only One Left"

On a screen in the café area, show a video of someone enacting Elijah's whine in response to God's question, 'What are you doing here, Elijah?' (1 Kings 19:10). Or get someone to act it out live. Include God's response from verse 11: 'Go out and stand on the mountain in the presence of the Lord, for the Lord is about to pass by.'

"The Lord is About to Pass By"

Invite everyone to return to the worship space where you started, because 'The Lord is about to pass by.'

You will need to re-create wind, earthquake and fire.

You may be able to find footage of strong winds from a DVD: for example, use the clip from *The Devil Wears Prada* where Miranda asks Andy to get her home from Hawaii, with a gale-force wind blowing outside the window. Use it with the sound turned down and some suitable music over the top. Or get people to flap large pieces of cloth; this will need some choreographing to make it seem like a powerful wind rather than some wafty breeze!

For the earthquake, you could use piles of cardboard boxes that get pushed over and thrown around by a few volunteers, or again look for film footage.

You could create your own film of a fire: light a bonfire and film it up close!

The music you choose for this section will help to set the tone. It needs to be loud, frenetic, busy, powerful.

Show or enact these three, one after the other, projecting words on a screen in between:

- The Lord was not in the wind
- The Lord was not in the earthquake
- The Lord was not in the fire.

Then stop the music, and allow people to settle into the silence. You could light a central candle. Project the words 'The Lord is in the gentle whisper' and 'Listen'. Give plenty of space for people to be simply quiet.

"Go Back the Way You Came"

Tell the rest of the story (verses 13–18).

Use this blessing,[11] shown over footage from the *Planet Earth: Deserts*

---

11 Jonny Baker

programme where water gushes in the desert and then flowers bloom. The blessing suits two voices reading alternate lines.

> *Go back the way you came...*
> *The desert and the parched land will be glad*
> *Go back the way you came...*
> *Water will gush forth in the wilderness and streams in the desert*
> *Go back the way you came...*
> *The burning sand will become a pool and thirsty ground bubbling springs.*
> *Go back the way you came...*
> *You're not the only one*
> *Go back the way you came...*
> *Build in time for rest, food and drink*
> *Go back the way you came...*
> *The wilderness will rejoice and blossom, like the crocus it will burst into*
>   *bloom*
> *Go back the way you came...*
> *Be strong. Do not fear. Your God will come.*
> *Go back the way you came...*
> *May gladness and joy overtake you and sorrow and sighing flee away*
> *Go back the way you came...*

CONNECTING WITH SCRIPTURE

The story of Elijah on Mount Horeb is found in 1 Kings 19:1–18.

HAND IT OVER

This way of engaging with the Bible has plenty of scope for young people to get involved in setting it up and running it. They can then use this idea for other Bible passages, creating experiences that help people to engage with the narrative.

Rewriting Psalm 23

WHAT HAPPENS?

People rewrite Psalm 23, by referring to a role that they fulfil for others, or that others fulfil for them, and exploring what this tells them about God.

EFFORT INVOLVED

MATERIALS NEEDED

- Paper and pens
- Bibles
- Copies of the worksheet
- You may like to play background music during this.

SOME THOUGHTS

Jesus describes himself as the good shepherd who lays down his life for his sheep. David said that the Lord was his shepherd. Those of us who are familiar with the Christian faith will probably link the two and think that there must be something very 'shepherdly' about God (if that's a word).

But we forget that when David wrote his psalm, the metaphor was new. And David was writing it after years of experience of being a shepherd himself. David picked a role that he knew all about, because it was a role he fulfilled for his sheep, and found parallels with the way that God cared for him, recognizing that God was a more perfect shepherd than he would ever be. It's perhaps another way of understanding the incarnate God. And I wonder what riches we can discover about God by examining what metaphors we can use from our own lives?

I rewrote Psalm 23 as 'The Lord is my mother...', which you can read on the following page, because that's one of the roles I fulfil in my life. I wasn't particularly saying anything about the gender of God, but found it really enlightening to consider how God mothers me as I mother my children, and to compare that with the way that my own mum mothered me.

HOW TO DO IT

Explain this idea to your group. Encourage them to think about the roles that they play in their lives, or roles that they know well because they have first-hand experience of them. They will need to choose a role that fits the relationship between them and God, so they may need to reverse the roles that they have first-hand experience of. So while it's not appropriate to write 'The Lord is my paper boy...', it could be enlightening to write 'The Lord is my employer...'

Other phrases that young people could choose to start their psalms include:

- 'The Lord is my brother (or sister)...' – after all, Jesus is described as our brother in Hebrews 2:11.
- 'The Lord is my mother (or father)...' – thinking about how God is a more perfect parent than their own.
- 'The Lord is my teacher...' – what does their experience of being a pupil tell them about what a perfect teacher is like?
- 'The Lord is my mentor...'
- 'The Lord is my coach...' – in what ways does God fulfil a role similar to that of a sports coach?

Stress that they are going to be exploring aspects of God's character; they're not saying that God is completely defined by this one metaphor. Remind them that they are not thinking about a particular person that they know, but about how God might fulfil this role perfectly for them.

You may like to use the photocopiable worksheet to help people structure their psalms. They don't have to follow the structure of the original psalm if they don't want to, but there will be something more striking about the end result if there is a familiar rhythm to the words.

Talk about the ideas that people come up with and about the paradoxical tension at the heart of any metaphor: that it will show us some aspects of God's character, but it won't encapsulate and define God completely. You can get people to read out their psalms at the end, or use them later in a worship service.

Connecting with Scripture
- Within the same chapter of Revelation Jesus is described as both a lion and a lamb – contrasting metaphors that don't seem to have much in common, but somehow reveal more of who Jesus is (Revelation 5:5–10).
- Moses describes God as a warrior: a metaphor that would have made sense to a people escaping from oppression, but that may lose its significance for those of us who are more remote from fighting and battles (Exodus 15:3).

Hand it Over

Another passage that lends itself well to this approach, although in a slightly different way, is Matthew 5:1–12: the Beatitudes. Invite young people to rewrite these according to what the world says makes someone happy or blessed or 'lucky'. In other words, they are writing the opposite of what Jesus said. Talk to them about their versions and get them to compare them with the original.

The Lord is my Mother

The Lord is my mother; I shall not be in want.
She makes me lie down in fresh clean sheets and tucks me in and kisses me
*   goodnight,*
and while I sleep she sorts everything out, ready for the morning.
She makes me cups of tea and ginger cake when I get home from school,
and shepherd's pie for supper, with plenty of fresh vegetables.
She leads me away from the TV to the kitchen table,
where we have space to talk without interruptions.
She listens to even the smallest of my worries and helps me get things in
*   perspective.*
She restores my soul.
She guides me through the mysteries of how to be a righteous woman, for her
*   name's sake.*

Even though I walk past the bus stop
where the big boys threaten me
and the bitchy girls laugh at me,
I will fear no evil, for you are with me.
Your strength beside me and your hand in mine,
they comfort and sustain me.

You prepare Sunday lunch for me in the presence of my enemies,
to remind me that I'll always have a place to belong.
You have every confidence in me and my future;
you are my champion and my biggest fan.
My life overflows with the love you have given me
from my very first breath to my first grey hair and beyond.
Surely goodness and mercy shall follow me all the days of my life,
and I shall dwell in the house of the Lord for ever.

Rewriting Psalm 23 – A Structure that May Help

The letters in normal type suggest phrases from the psalm that you might like to leave as they are. The comments on the right get you to think about what you might include, so that you mirror the structure of the original psalm. Have a copy of the original psalm open in front of you, to compare.

The LORD is my _____ ; I shall not want	*How might this person make sure you get enough rest?*
He/she guides me....	*What do they give you guidance in?*
Even though I walk...	*Where are the dangerous or dark places that you have to go? How would someone fulfilling this role protect you? How would you know they are supporting you, even when they're not there?*
I will fear no evil for...	*How might this person celebrate your achievements or make a fuss of you? How could they show their confidence in you?*
You...	*Feel free to add in more ideas, even if they're not in the original psalm.*
Surely goodness and love will follow me all the days of my life, and I will dwell in the house of the Lord for ever.	*Why not finish off in the same way as Psalm 23?*

A Different Perspective

What Happens?

A Bible story is retold from the point of view of different characters in it, in a way that helps people to engage with key questions.

Effort Involved

Materials Needed

- Copies of the scripts on the following pages
- Paper and pens
- You may decide you want to add some props.

Some Thoughts

Some Bible stories are so familiar that we lose some of what they have to offer us. We think we know the punchline, so we switch off. Or we have heard a passage taught in a certain way so many times that we decide we know what it means.

The beauty of many Bible passages is that we will find different aspects of the truth in them, depending on what we need to hear from God at different times. This way of presenting a well-known story unlocks some key questions, and allows the word of God to penetrate our familiarity.

How to Do it

Think about how the different characters will each tell their part of the story. Are there simple props that would help them play their parts? How can you arrange the lighting and the seats to help people to focus on them? Get people to discuss this in small groups; it may help to divide them up before the start. Give them pens and paper, to record any thoughts and questions that they have.

Get someone to read the story of the Good Samaritan from Luke 10:25–37.

The man who got beaten up should then deliver his side of the story. Next, get people into small groups to discuss the question that he ends with: 'Why did the priest ignore me?' Allow plenty of time for discussion.

Then the Levite tells his part of the story. In small groups, people discuss the question that he ends with: 'What did that bloke have to do with me?'

Finally, the innkeeper's wife tells her story. In small groups, people discuss the question that she ends with: 'Why did the Samaritan stop and help that man?'

Then call everyone together and discuss the experience. Get feedback from the groups, and talk about their questions and comments. Encourage people to apply their insights to themselves. Who in the story did they identify with most? What is God saying to them through it? What is Jesus inviting them to be, or to do, in response to this passage?

CONNECTING WITH SCRIPTURE
Jesus tells the story of the Good Samaritan in Luke 10:25–37.

HAND IT OVER
Get young people involved in acting out the parts. If they can learn them off by heart, so much the better. Once they have experienced this way of engaging with a Bible story, they can use it with other passages. Getting them to work on scripts and then talking those through with them can be a really valuable learning experience.

The Man Who Got Beaten Up

I've done the journey a few times before and never had any trouble. You hear about these things happening. I knew there was a risk, but you never think it's going to happen to you.

I didn't see it coming at all; I had no sense that anyone was watching me. I was striding along, thinking about the guy I was going to be meeting in Jericho, when someone jumped on me from behind. He was a big bloke; there was no way I could stay on my feet, and then once I was down, they laid into me, kicking and punching me. Someone hit me with something hard – I didn't see what it was. I was trying to cover my head with my hands, longing for it to stop, praying to God, thinking about my family. And then I passed out.

When I came to, it was hot. My mouth was parched and full of dust. I could hardly move my tongue. One eye was swollen shut and I could just about see out of the other one. I tried to get up, but my legs were like jelly. I knew they would have taken my money, but I wasn't worried about that – I just wanted to live.

I lay there for what seemed like hours, drifting in and out of consciousness, willing someone to walk down the road. And then I heard footsteps – what a relief! I tried to sit up some more; I tried to wave. I could see he was a priest, and I started thanking God that help had come at last. I tried to call out, but my throat was so dry I don't know if I made any sense.

The footsteps got quicker, and then went past. He didn't even look at me; just kept his head down and kept walking. I couldn't believe it. I called out. He can't have missed me; he must have seen I was there. But he just walked past me – left me on my own. That was when I cried for the first time. I felt like I'd lost all hope.

I've been thinking about that ever since. Why did that priest ignore me?

The Levite

I'm in the doghouse – which is why I'm out here in the garden, having a drink and waiting for my wife and daughters to calm down. They weren't even there! I don't know why they're so up in arms.

It started over supper, where we were all talking about what we'd done during the day. I told them about my journey to Jericho, but that's not very exciting, is it? Hot dusty road, surrounded by hot dusty hills and hot dusty fields. I thought I'd spice it up a bit and mention the highlights of the journey – the tree that was bent over by the side of the road; the number of times I recited the Ten Commandments as I walked; that bloke by the side of the road who'd been attacked by robbers.

And that's when they started having a go. I wish I'd kept my mouth shut. They obviously thought I should have done something – but what? I'd thought it was a bundle of rags at first; something someone had thrown away. As I got closer I could see it was a body, but I had no way of knowing whether he was alive or dead. It was hot; I was on foot; I didn't have anything with me that I could use to help him; and besides, I didn't want to go and touch a dead body, did I? That would have been very inconvenient.

But my wife and daughters had other ideas. I should have stopped, apparently. I should have done something, although they didn't say what. They were outraged that I was so heartless and cold!

But I still think that I did the right thing. There were bound to be other people making that journey who were better placed to help than me. Surely it wasn't my problem? Tell me, what did that bloke have to do with me?

The Innkeeper's Wife

I'm so glad to get the weight off my feet! It's been busy in here tonight. I'm not complaining, mind – business is business. But it's only when you sit down that you realize how tired you are. There's been people coming and going all day, and then that injured man needed extra attention. Ruth's been looking after him, not me, but it just means there's been more for me to do. Still, she says he seems better this evening. It looked touch and go when he arrived last night, on the back of that guy's donkey.

I still can't quite get my head round that. It's not that unusual to see people who've been beaten up and robbed; it happens several times a year on that road. But we were amazed when they turned up at the door – saw it straight away. He was a Samaritan, you see, and the injured guy was one of us – Jewish. Matthew, my husband, was very professional – didn't comment or anything, just found them rooms and sorted out what they needed. But as soon as they were out of sight, we talked about it at great length. Normally those Samaritans keep themselves to themselves – well, that's only natural, isn't it? There's loads of history there; we just don't have anything to do with them.

But this one was different. Seems that he stopped and helped this guy, brought him here, and then this morning gave Matthew some money so that we would look after him – amazing! He'll be back in a few days, and I'd really like to ask him – why on earth did you stop and help that man?

Get into Character

What Happens?

Assign characters from a Bible story to each member of the group. They then have a conversation 'in role' that helps them explore different aspects of the story.

Effort Involved

Materials Needed

- copies of the character cards from the following pages
- copies of Luke 8:40–56, printed out from www.biblegateway.com; or use Bibles

Some Thoughts

This is another exercise that can help young people to engage more deeply with a Bible story by getting them to imagine they are characters within it. Creating space for imagination and wondering can be enlightening, as you consider aspects of a story different from those that leap off the page.

Inevitably, some of this will be subjective; you're asking twenty-first-century Western teenagers to imagine what it was like to be part of an event in first-century Palestine. Not everything that is said will be relevant or illuminating; but a lot of it will. Debriefing the activity afterwards is very important, as is having one leader who can play the part of someone in the crowd. As they don't have a key role in the story, they will be able to listen to what others are saying. Their role in the debrief is not to 'police' what went on, but to enable people to consider whether what happened in the role play is true to the story and helps us to understand the word of God better.

How to Do it

There are eight key characters in this story: Jairus, his wife, his daughter, the woman with the bleeding, Peter, James, John and the servant. (Have you noticed that the women – like the employee – are not named in the passage? What might that say about the culture?) If you have more than eight people in your group, others can play parts as mourners, or people in the crowd. If you have fewer than eight people, leave out the parts of James, John and then the servant – but don't do the story with any fewer than five people. I have chosen not to give someone the character of Jesus, but you may feel differently. Give your leaders roles so that they are fully engaged, bearing in mind the point made above about someone playing the role of someone in the crowd. Brief the leaders to get conversations going and to ask lots of questions.

Hand out character cards to each member of the group. Invite them to read Luke 8:40–56, looking out for what it says about their character. Encourage them to imagine how their character might have felt at different points during the story. What might they have been thinking? What was going on that they didn't know about?

Then get people to circulate and talk about the story in role. An opening question that anyone can use is 'What have you been doing today?' Get people to explore what happened and why; how people felt; what they were thinking.

Let this run for as long as the discussions continue. Then invite everyone to come out of role. It might be helpful to signal a change in emphasis by having refreshments at this point. Then get people to debrief the activity. What did they discover? What questions did this activity raise? Why is this story in the Bible? How does it apply to us? What is Jesus inviting us to do or to be in response to this passage?

Connecting with Scripture

The healings of Jairus' daughter and of the woman with bleeding are found in Luke 8:40–56, Matthew 9:18–26 and Mark 5:22–43.

Hand it Over

This is another activity that requires people to be fully engaged. Allocate the parts carefully. Don't simply give the biggest parts to the most vocal members of your group; this could be an opportunity for quieter people to shine. And giving chattier people smaller parts could potentially allow those parts to develop further.

[Each of the following character sketches needs to be set out on a separate card that can be cut out and handed to people.]

Jairus

You are a leader in the local synagogue: well respected and strong. Your daughter, Esther, is ill – in fact, she is dying and you are desperate for help. You've heard about Jesus and the healing he has done. You go to find him and ask him to heal your daughter. You want to get him back to Esther as quickly as you can; you're annoyed at all the crowds getting in the way.

Esther

You are 12 years old, the only daughter of Jairus and Anna. You used to enjoy playing with your friends and learning things from your dad, but you've been ill for a while now. And recently you've begun to feel worse. You don't want to worry your mum and dad too much – you can see that they're really anxious – but you feel so weak and helpless.

Anna

Your only daughter, Esther, is desperately ill. As a last resort your husband, Jairus, has gone to find Jesus, the man who is said to be able to heal. Jairus is a leader in the local synagogue, a powerful and important man, but now desperate to see your daughter well again. You don't know what to do, other than sit by Esther's side, waiting and praying.

Tabitha

You've been ill for years now. It's embarrassing, but you bleed all the time. You've spent all your money on doctors. You've tried all kinds of cures, but nothing has worked. Everyone keeps away from you; they don't want to be made unclean. You've heard about this man called Jesus. People say he can heal. You wonder if that's true. You wonder whether, if you sneak up, some of that would rub off on you without you disturbing him.

Peter

Jesus is so popular these days – crowds follow him everywhere. It gets frustrating; there's so little time for you and the other disciples to talk to him. Still, you wouldn't be anywhere else. You want to learn all you can from him.

James

Jesus is so popular these days – crowds follow him everywhere. It gets frustrating; there's so little time for you and the other disciples to talk to him. Still, you wouldn't be anywhere else. You want to learn all you can from him.

John

Jesus is so popular these days – crowds follow him everywhere. It gets frustrating; there's so little time for you and the other disciples to talk to him. Still, you wouldn't be anywhere else. You want to learn all you can from him.

Festus

You have worked for Jairus and Anna for the last 20 years. You are a respected member of the household: more of a trusted friend than a servant. You know how worried he is about his daughter and you wish there was something you could do to help. (You turn up in verse 49.)

Member of the Crowd

You've heard so much about this man Jesus. Apparently he can heal people. Somebody said that he has even raised someone from the dead! But you need to see it with your own eyes – which is why you're going to follow him, to see what happens.

Mourner

You have known the family for years. You've kept in touch with Esther's illness and have offered help and comfort to Jairus and Anna, her parents. But now it's happened. Esther has died. It's hard to take it in; but you feel you need to be there to mourn and to support Jairus and Anna.

Holy Reading

WHAT HAPPENS?

People draw and write in response to a passage of the Bible that is read slowly a number of times.

EFFORT INVOLVED

● ○ ○

MATERIALS NEEDED

- Paper and pens
- Bible.

SOME THOUGHTS

Lectio Divina is a practice that has come from the Benedictine tradition and is described in detail in the 'Team' section of this book, on page 169. Lectio Divina means 'holy reading'; it is a slow, prayerful way of reading the Bible.

Lectio Divina is enhanced when people have a good knowledge of the Bible and can bring to it a measure of maturity in understanding Scripture. Some people worry that it is too subjective a practice to use with young people, but if done with care it gives them a great opportunity really to listen to the word of God and to linger with it. Discussing it afterwards gives you an opportunity to provide guidance on God's word, and gives you insights into their understanding of the Christian faith.

HOW TO DO IT

Choose a passage of Scripture to read to the group. Below, I suggest you read Matthew 20:29–34 – the story of two blind men being healed by Jesus – but do choose your own, depending on the needs and stages of development of your group. Keep it short. They may find it easier to relate to a narrative passage.

Adapt the suggested text below to suit your group. You will also need to judge how long the periods of silence should be. You could read the passage fewer times, if appropriate for your group.

Invite young people to find a space where they can be comfortable and can draw and write in private. Make sure everyone has a piece of paper and a pen, and knows where to get extra paper if they need it. Tell people that you are going to read a passage from the Bible a number of times, with short pauses of silence in between each reading. Each time, you will suggest something for them to draw or write in the silence. If you're using the text below, make sure they know what a mind map is. At the end, you will call everyone together and you'll have a chance to discuss what they have drawn, written and been thinking about.

> *I'm going to read you a story about Jesus from the Bible and I want you to listen out for a word or a phrase that stands out for you. There will be a short period of silence after the reading, when I'd like you to write your word or phrase on your paper over and over again, thinking about its meaning.*
>
> Read Matthew 20:29–34 slowly and carefully.
>
> *Write your word or phrase on your paper over and over again.*
>
> (Leave a short period of silence.)
>
> *I'm going to read the same story again. This time, in the silence, write your word one more time, and then draw a mind map to write down all the thoughts and images that come to mind around that word.*
>
> Read Matthew 20:29–34 again, slowly and carefully.
>
> *Now create a mind map of your word.*
>
> (Leave a short period of silence.)
>
> *I'm going to read the same story again. This time, in the silence, I want you to draw on the paper a figure that represents you. Then write or draw around it how this story affects you, right now.*
>
> Read Matthew 20:29–34 slowly and carefully.
>
> *Draw how this relates to you.*
>
> (Leave a short period of silence.)

I'm going to read the same story one last time. This time in the silence I want you to write down any questions you have about the passage.

Read Matthew 20:29–34 slowly and carefully.

Write down your questions.

(Leave a short period of silence.)

Invite people to bring their attention back to the room. Then invite feedback on that experience, encouraging people to share what they have written and answering any questions that they might have.

Connecting with Scripture

God tells the Israelites to talk about God's commandments with their children 'When you sit at home and when you walk along the road, when you lie down and when you get up.' This exercise gives young people a chance to think about God's word for themselves and to have something to bring to those conversations (Deuteronomy 6:4–9).

Hand it Over

Encourage young people to use a similar process when they read the Bible themselves, using Bible notes. The temptation can be to race through the passage and to read the notes hoping for a funny anecdote. Suggest that they read the passage through three times, slowly, with a space in between to reflect on what they have read and to chew it over.

Make sure people have suitable versions of the Bible to read at home. Show them the Biblegateway website (www.biblegateway.com), so they can try different versions to see which one is appropriate for them.

Cross it Out

What Happens?

People use black marker pens to cross out all references to the poor and needy in a Bible passage, as a way of highlighting what the Bible says about the poor.

Effort Involved

● ◑ ◉

Materials Needed

- Bible passages printed from www.biblegateway.com: for details, see below
- Black marker pens.

Some Thoughts

My son bought a hoody with a slogan printed on the inside next to the zip. It said, 'Our lives begin to end the day we become silent,' and it really bugged me. What did it mean? Why was it there? Who had said it? As someone who values silence, I couldn't agree with it – I think life becomes richer the day we learn to be silent! It led to some interesting conversations with my son, who understood it to mean that we die a little if we stop expressing ourselves, or our creativity is stifled – something that I could endorse.

And then one day I saw the quote on a website. It said, 'Our lives begin to end the day we become silent about the things that matter,' and it was attributed to Martin Luther King. And suddenly it all made sense! Knowing the full quote and who had said it, I could understand why someone might want to reproduce it. The addition of the missing few words made all the difference; but if I'd never seen the incomplete slogan, I doubt that I would have paid much attention to it.

This activity gets people to destroy all references to a particular topic in a Bible passage, and then read it, so that when you look back at the complete passage, the thing that strikes you is what you had taken out. Following the example of Jim Wallis, I've chosen passages where you'll invite people to cross out references to the poor and needy; but you can choose any topic.

How to Do it

Print out the following passages from Bible Gateway – www.biblegateway. com – using your preferred version. The Contemporary English Version has a low reading age, which may make it more suitable for some groups. You'll hand one passage to each pair in your group, and you'll need two copies of each passage, so that people can compare their crossed-out versions back to the original.

- Isaiah 58:1–10
- Matthew 25:31–46
- Deuteronomy 15:1–11
- Luke 4:14–21.

Add further relevant passages, if you think your group can cope with them, or use only one or two, if that would be more appropriate.

Get people into pairs and hand one Bible passage to each pair, keeping back another set of the same passages. Hand out the marker pens and invite them to cross out every reference to people who are poor and in need, and to how we should treat them. For a start, this will get people reading the passage quite closely!

Once they have done this, invite everyone who had the Isaiah passage to read out what they have left. Discuss any discrepancies – should any more be crossed out by some people? Then do the same for the other passages.

Discuss what people have heard. What is each passage about? Does it make any sense? Can they summarize it in one or two sentences?

Then hand out the unmarked set of readings, so that everyone has a full copy of their text. Invite them to read both passages again. Then read them out loud in the group – the edited passages, followed by the full versions.

What was lost when you just read the edited passages? How would you sum up the full passages in just one or two sentences? How might the missing words affect our actions and the way we live our lives?

You could go on to discuss why some people ignore some parts of the Bible, and the importance of studying and understanding God's word.

Connecting with Scripture

Jesus said that he came to fulfil the Law and Prophets, not to abolish them. We can't discard bits of the Bible that we don't like! (Matthew 5:17–20)

CHAPTER 4
Contemplative

The word 'contemplative' means being in the 'temple', the place where God dwells. Contemplative prayer is about resting attentively within the presence of God, choosing to be still and quiet and to recognize the presence of God around us and within us. It sounds challenging and super-spiritual; in fact, it is one of the things that can keep us grounded and connected to God in our busy lives. For a full and inspiring exploration of how this flavour of prayer and worship can shape you, the youth ministry that you are involved in and the young people that you work with, you need to read *Contemplative Youth Ministry* by Mark Yaconelli (SPCK). You need to explore and experience contemplative prayer for yourself, before you launch into it with young people.

Young people are so used to being entertained, connected and stimulated that being still and quiet can feel alien and uncomfortable. If they allow themselves to enter into a contemplative place, though, it can provide a lifeline from the stress and strain that they are under: a space to be themselves and to encounter God. It is wise to talk in advance about how they might find stillness and silence, and to find ways to ease them into and out of the experience, gradually increasing the amount of time that they spend within it.

There are many traditions of contemplative prayer within the Christian church. The activities that follow draw on some of these in a way that is accessible to young people. Pay careful attention to the environment in which you lead these activities, minimizing distractions and creating a space that is conducive to stillness.

Breathing Prayer

What Happens?

This prayer invites people to become aware of their breathing and to use that as a means to be open to God and to become still.

Effort Involved

● ○ ○

Materials Needed

You may like to play some quiet instrumental music in the background.

Some Thoughts

At the creation of the world, Genesis tells us that God breathed into a clay figure and it became a living human being. Without thinking, we take thousands of breaths each day, a continuation of that first breath that God invested in that first person. Focusing on your breath as you pray makes you aware of a rhythm and stillness to your being. And it's a technique that is easy to reproduce, wherever you are.

How to Do It

Invite people to find a space and make themselves comfortable. Some may like to sit on the floor against a wall; some may like to lie down; others will want to sit on a chair. Encourage people to sit or lie with their backs supported, their legs uncrossed and their feet flat on the floor. Invite them to close their eyes. Read this prayer slowly and rhythmically, giving time for a breath in and out in after each phrase.

Sit comfortably and be still.
Enjoy the peace of this place.
As you relax your body, gently become aware of your breathing...
Breathe a little more deeply, a little more slowly.

Breathe in the spirit of God; breathe out worry.
Breathe in the love of God; breathe out loneliness.
Breathe in the acceptance of God; breathe out the need to impress.
Breathe in the presence of God; breathe out all that troubles you.

Breathe in peace; breathe out tension.
Breathe in love; breathe out hate.
Breathe in acceptance; breathe out rejection.
Breathe in forgiveness; breathe out blame.
Breathe in life; breathe out death.
Breathe in trust; breathe out fear.

Breathe in; breathe out;
Breathe in; breathe out.

This prayer can lead into a time of stillness, or of spoken prayer, or sung worship. Make sure that you tell the young people what's going to happen next. If there will be a time of silence, guide them as to how long this will be, and remember to bring them out of it when it is over.

CONNECTING WITH SCRIPTURE

- When God created man, God formed him from earth and then breathed into his nostrils, and the man became a living being (Genesis 2:7).
- Isaiah reminds us that God 'created the heavens and stretched them out... spread out the earth with all that springs from it... gives breath to its people, and life to those who walk on it' (Isaiah 42:5).

HAND IT OVER

Young people can write their own versions of what to focus on as they breathe in and breathe out. Having experienced this way of praying, they may like to lead the group in a similar prayer themselves.

Examen

What Happens?

The examen is an Ignatian exercise that invites us to look back over our day and ask two simple questions: for what moment am I most grateful? And for what moment am I least grateful?[12]

Effort Involved

Materials Needed

- Large sheets of paper
- Pens
- Lemons
- Breadsticks and honey
- Dishes to put these in
- You may like to play some instrumental music in the background.

Some Thoughts

Ignatius of Loyola was a Spanish nobleman who was born at the end of the fifteenth century. He was brought up a Catholic, but as a young man preferred fighting, gambling and women. During a battle at Pamplona he was hit in the legs by a cannonball and was sent back to his castle to recover.

He spent his time in daydreams of what he would do when he recovered – of the courageous adventures he would go on, the battles he would win and the beautiful women he would impress. But he grew bored with that and asked for some books to read. The only books available were a Life of Christ and some biographies of the saints.

Reading these books made him decide to follow Jesus and he embarked on a new set of daydreams, where he was outdoing the saints in their devotion to Christ. He imagined himself fasting for longer, serving the poor more faithfully, spending more hours in prayer and sacrificing more pleasures.

He alternated between the two types of daydreams and then noticed something profound. The daydreams about battles and adventures left

---

12 An excellent book that explains more about the examen and how to respond to consolation and desolation is *Sleeping with Bread*, by Dennis Linn, Sheila Fabricant Linn and Matthew Linn, published by Paulist Press.

him feeing bored, empty and sad. The daydreams about serving Jesus left him excited, hopeful and energized. This insight led him to develop the practice called the examen, identifying the moments in our day for which we are most grateful and least grateful.

These questions enable us to identify moments of consolation – those moments when we have been aware of God's presence and have felt most alive – and moments of desolation – where we have felt drained of life and have struggled to see God. Ignatius taught that God would speak through these insights and, as we respond to them, we would learn to discern God's call on our lives.

This is a simple version of the examen that can be used with young people and helps them to recognize the presence of God in their lives in moments of joy and sorrow.

How to Do it

Cut the lemons into slices and put them, the honey and the breadsticks in three separate dishes. On a large sheet of paper, write the word 'bitter' in the centre of one side and write the word 'sweet' in the centre of the other side. If you have a large group, you may need to prepare more sheets, so that a small group can gather round each. You'll start with the side that says 'sweet'.

Remind people that God is with them and that God loves them. Pray, thanking God for God's presence and asking God to help the group in this activity. You may feel that it is appropriate to use a stilling exercise, to encourage the group to settle into God's presence.

Invite the young people to shut their eyes and think back over the last week. Get them to go over the things that they have done, the people that they have spent time with, the places they have been. Encourage them to think about the different feelings they have experienced: the highs and lows of the last week. Allow a bit of time for this, and play some suitable music to help people to relax into it.

Then ask people to think about this question:

- For what moment in the last week am I most grateful?

Invite them to draw or write something on the sheet that represents this moment of gratitude. Invite them to eat some honey and breadsticks and to thank God that God was with them in that moment. Invite them to consider what it was about that moment that was so special. What opportunity does it give them to grow?

Then turn the sheets over and invite people to think about the second question of the examen:

- For what moment in the last week am I least grateful?

Again, invite them to draw or write something on the sheet that represents this moment. Acknowledge that this question may raise uncomfortable feelings, but encourage them to stay with it. Invite them to eat a slice of lemon and to thank God that God was with them in that moment, even though they may not have been aware of that. Invite them to consider what it was about that moment that was difficult. What opportunity does it give them to grow?

Close this time with some prayer, or sung worship. Invite people to ask God how they should respond to those moments. Make sure that people know who they can talk to, if they need to take anything further.

CONNECTING WITH SCRIPTURE

In Psalm 23, David recognizes God as being with him in both the peaceful green pastures and the valley of the shadow of death.

HAND IT OVER

The examen is a wonderful tool to use to discern God's calling on our lives. If you mentor any young people, encourage them to do this regularly and to make a note in their journals of their moments of most and least gratitude, so that you can talk about them together when you meet.

This is also a really useful exercise to do as a team, looking back over the youth ministry you have worked at together and identifying moments of consolation and desolation. It does require a commitment to be honest with each other and to grow together as a team, so is not to be undertaken lightly!

Stilling

What Happens?

Lead people in a meditation that encourages them to let go of the things on their minds and become still before God.

Effort Involved

Materials Needed

You may like to play some instrumental music in the background.

Some Thoughts

It takes practice to be fully present in prayer. Often, when you stop to pray, 1,001 things stream through your mind: things that need to be done, people that you need to talk to, what's for supper tonight, what's on TV afterwards... The harder you try not to think about them, the more persistently they swim into view. This meditation invites people to name the things that are on their minds, then deliberately to put them down and leave them behind as they prepare to meet Jesus in prayer.

How to Do it

Invite people to find a space and make themselves comfortable, with their eyes closed. Read these words slowly, leaving pauses where appropriate to give time for people to use their imaginations.

> *Make yourself comfortable, with your back supported and your feet flat on the floor. Become aware of your body, and invite every part of it to relax.*
> *Allow your breathing to become slower and deeper.*
> *Imagine yourself holding in your arms things that represent what's on your mind – a computer might represent your homework; a photo might represent a relationship; a bag might represent your paper round...*
> *Perhaps you're holding just one thing, but it's very heavy. Perhaps your arms are so full that it's hard to hold onto everything. Take a few moments to realize what those things are and what you are holding. If it helps you to visualize it, hold your arms out in front of you. How much are you carrying? How much is it weighing you down?*

Then, one by one, put those things down around your feet. In your mind, name them and let go of them, one by one. Put them down. Let them go. Take your time.

Imagine yourself stepping over those things and walking away from them. Leave them behind. Take a deep breath as you move away. Imagine yourself walking tall, with your arms completely empty. How does it feel to be free of those things?

You are going to meet Jesus in a safe place. Imagine what that place looks and feels like.

Jesus is here with you – you might not be able to see him, but he is here. Sit down in this place of safety and make yourself at home.

You are welcome. You are loved. You are listened to.

This then needs to lead into something: a period of silence; space to reflect on a Bible passage; some more structured worship. Make sure that people know what's going to happen and how long it will last before you begin the exercise.

CONNECTING WITH SCRIPTURE
- Peter tells us to cast our anxiety on God, because God cares for us (1 Peter 5:7).
- Jesus teaches us not to worry about what we'll eat, drink or wear, but to seek first God's kingdom (Matthew 6:25–34).

HAND IT OVER
Invite young people to write a meditation that leads from a place of busyness and noise to a place of stillness. Get them to think of the noisiest, most frantic place that they know, and then the most peaceful. What is the journey from one to the other? How might they change on that journey? What outward transformation could mirror what needs to happen for them to be still before God?

Praying Without Words

What Happens?

People are guided to use art as a way of expressing in prayer what it is difficult to put into words.

Effort Involved

Materials Needed

- Large sheets of paper, enough for one each
- Art materials: paints, markers, pastels, crayons
- You may like to play some instrumental music in the background.

Some Thoughts

Sometimes it can be difficult to find the words to pray – when a child is very ill, or we see thousands of people facing starvation, or we hear about terrorism and conflict. We know that we want to see God intervene, to bring healing, reconciliation and peace, but it can be hard to find the right words for complex or painful situations.

If we've already prayed many times about the same thing, sometimes we can just run out of words. We know we need to be persistent in prayer, but we don't want to keep repeating the same phrases. This guided prayer time will help people to pray when they don't know how to put the longings of their hearts into words.

How to Do it

Invite everyone to find a space where they are comfortable and have enough room. Ask them to think about the issue that they want to bring to God. It may be that everyone in the group is affected by the same tragedy – maybe someone you all know is very ill, or suffering, or there is a local issue that you all feel strongly about. At other times, perhaps each individual will be thinking about something different.

Read Romans 8:26, 27 (quoted here in NIV) and then pray out loud on behalf of the group:

'In the same way, the Spirit helps us in our weakness. We do not know what we ought to pray for, but the Spirit himself intercedes for us with

groans that words cannot express. And he who searches our hearts knows the mind of the Spirit, because the Spirit intercedes for the saints in accordance with God's will.'

Lord, you know the deepest desires of our hearts. Hear our prayer, even when we have no words to pray.

Invite people to draw or paint the situation that they want to pray for. These drawings don't have to be exact representations – they can use colour or shapes to express their feelings. As they draw, encourage people to be aware of God's presence with them as they are honest about how they feel. They may find it helpful to repeat a simple phrase to themselves as they paint, such as 'Lord Jesus', or 'Help me, Lord', to remind themselves that they are praying and that God is with them. Let people know when it is time to move on by saying something like: 'You have one more minute to finish that part of your painting.'

Then prompt people to think about who God is, and God's power to heal and reconcile, and encourage them to use the art materials to represent God in their picture. Again, they can use colour and shapes and should be honest about their feelings. If God seems remote from the situation they want to pray for, they can paint in the corner of the paper – or even on a different sheet. If they know God is at work, they can paint around or over their initial artwork.

Finally, ask people to draw or paint what they long for God to do in this situation: perhaps a picture of a person healed or of people reconciled. Colour can be used really powerfully in these paintings: perhaps moving from darker greys and blues that express despair and pain, through yellow or gold that represents God's love, to strong reds and purples that speak of healing – although, of course, every painting will be unique, and people may choose completely different colours.

Conclude the prayer time by thanking God that God has been present with you and has heard the cries of your hearts and the groans that words cannot express. People can take their pictures home to remind them of this time of prayer, or, if appropriate, they can be left on the walls of the room where you meet.

CONNECTING WITH SCRIPTURE

When we don't know how to pray, the Spirit intercedes for us. God helps us to pray to God (Romans 8:26, 27).

Hand it Over

Young people with artistic gifts may find this a very liberating way of praying, being able to express the things on their hearts without having to put them into words.

Block of Ice

What Happens?

People place lit nightlights under a block of ice while they pray, to remind them to be persistent in prayer.

Effort Involved

Materials Needed

- A large block of ice: you need to start preparing this well in advance
- Net or mesh bag
- Rope
- Waterproof covering
- Bowl
- Large candle, nightlights
- Matches.

Some Thoughts

We live in a world where we expect instant results. If a web page takes more than three seconds to load, we click on in frustration. We're used to tools and gadgets that deliver us what we want almost as soon as we've decided we want it.

But sometimes when we come to pray, we need to be patient and persistent. Jesus told the parable of the persistent widow, who kept going to the unjust judge to demand justice. Eventually the judge gave in, because he was so fed up with her bothering him. God is not hard-hearted and unjust, like the judge. God will bring justice for God's people, but sometimes it takes time, and we need to pray and not give up.

We also need reminding that our prayers are significant, that they do make a difference – not because it's we who are praying, but because of whom we pray to. When we pray about global poverty, for natural disasters, for people caught up in persecution or terrorism, it's tempting to think that nothing happens. But just as a single nightlight will make a block of ice melt just a little bit faster, and a stroke with sandpaper will make a rough stick just a little bit smoother, so our prayers do contribute to the work of God's kingdom.

How to Do it

Create a block of ice by freezing water in a large container: it is easiest if you freeze it in layers, an inch or two at a time, rather than trying to freeze it all in one go.

Put the ice in a net or mesh bag and hang it from a beam or hook in the ceiling, using the rope. The ice needs to be between five and eight inches from the floor. Put a waterproof covering on the floor underneath the ice, to protect it. Angle the block of ice in the net so that drips from the melting water will fall from one end, rather than all along the bottom. Put a bowl underneath to catch the drips, so you don't end up with a large puddle.

Set up and light the large candle nearby and put the unlit nightlights around it.

Tell the story of the persistent widow from Luke 18:1–8. It's about an unjust judge who didn't fear God or care about people. A widow kept coming to him, asking him for justice. He refused to listen to her, but she kept on coming back with the same request. In the end, he got fed up with her and made sure that she got justice, so that she wouldn't bother him any longer! Explain that Jesus told this story to encourage people to pray and not give up. Make it clear that God is the opposite of the unjust judge: God is not hard-hearted and does listen to us. Ask people to think of something they have been praying about for a long time – perhaps for a friend or a member of their family to come to know Christ. Alternatively, they could think of a difficult situation that needs prayer – where it is hard to see how and when God might answer.

Invite people to reflect on the ice. It is cold and hard and unyielding. And yet even a small amount of warmth will help to melt the ice more quickly. Ask people to pray for the situation on their mind and, as they do so, to take a nightlight and light it from the big candle. They can place their nightlight under the block of ice to help it melt. As they look at the flames underneath the ice, they can continue to pray, asking God to soften people's hearts, to transform cold into warmth.

You could encourage people to get into groups of two or three and talk to each other about the situations they have prayed for, to encourage one another and to pray for one another.

Alternative – Sanding Sticks

As an alternative idea on this same theme of being persistent in prayer, have a display of logs with some smaller sticks or kindling around them and some pieces of sandpaper. The logs aren't essential to this prayer idea – they just look good! Introduce a subject or theme for prayer, or ask people to think of something they have been praying about for a long time. As people pray, invite them to take a stick and use the sandpaper to sand away the rough bark or outside layer of the stick. To make the stick really smooth takes a lot of work. They can take the stick and sandpaper home with them and keep sanding their stick as they continue to pray over the coming weeks.

Connecting with Scripture

Jesus tells the parable of the persistent widow to remind us that we need to pray and not give up (Luke 18:1–8).

Hand it Over

Young people will love being involved in setting up something like this, and will usually have creative ideas for how to hang the ice, or display the logs.

Outdoor Prayer

WHAT HAPPENS?

People are given a folded sheet of paper. They find a space on their own and unfold the instructions one by one, being guided into stillness and prayer.[13]

EFFORT INVOLVED

MATERIALS NEEDED

- Copies of the photocopiable sheet
- Space outdoors and good weather
- If it's been raining recently, people may want something waterproof to sit on.

SOME THOUGHTS

Most of us, if we're honest, aren't very good at silence. We like noise, people around us, being busy, doing – rather than just sitting and being. Young people, in particular, are so used to being connected and active every minute of every day, of having competing demands on their attention, that it can feel awkward and strange to sit and do nothing. And so we don't give ourselves time to settle, to be still, to listen for what God might be saying to us. How much do we miss because we're afraid of silence?

This activity guides people into stillness and prayer through instructions on a sheet of paper that they reveal slowly one by one.

HOW TO DO IT

This is a great activity to do at a residential event, or, if there is not enough open space where you usually meet, take people to a park. If you want to do this in the winter instead, you could adapt these instructions and make your own indoor version. Get people to spread out inside the church, and pick out appropriate things that they can focus on.

Make enough copies of the sheet for everyone to have one. Fold them up, from the bottom, along the lines, so that people can unfold them from the top, revealing one instruction at a time.

Gather everyone together and explain the activity. Tell them that they

---

13 Brian Spurling, Urban Saints

need to reveal instruction 1 in a moment and then follow it. Each time they have finished an instruction, they unfold the paper to reveal the next one. They read it and then take time to do what it says (rather than reading it and trying to do it at the same time). Encourage them to linger on each instruction, not to rush through them.

Tell them about any restrictions there may be on where they can go – you may want to make sure they stay within sight of you – and tell them what to do when they have finished the last instruction. Perhaps they could come back inside, to share a hot chocolate and to chat about how they found the activity.

CONNECTING WITH SCRIPTURE
- Elijah found that God was not in the noise and drama of the earthquake, the fire or the wind, but in the gentle whisper (1 Kings 19:11–13).
- 'Be still, and know that I am God' (Psalm 46:10).

HAND IT OVER
Young people can take these sheets away and use them again, adding different Bible passages to read. Or they could write similar instructions for each other, so that there is an element of surprise in them.

1   Find somewhere you can be in a space on your own, away from everyone else.

2   Lie down on your back. Place your hands flat on the floor. Take ten deep breaths, in and out, and feel yourself slowing down.

3   What can you hear? Listen carefully and name the sounds around you.

4   What noise is going on inside you? Name your worries, or the things on your mind, and imagine putting them to one side.

5   Sit and grow used to the silence around you, and ask God to meet you in it.

6   Find a leaf, a flower, or a blade of grass and take a close look at it.

7   Think about the creation around you: trees, flowers and grass growing and changing throughout the year, in silence. Imagine what this place looks like through the different seasons – winter, spring, summer and autumn.

8   The Bible says: 'The basic reality of God is plain enough. Open your eyes and there it is! By taking a long and thoughtful look at what God has created, people have always been able to see what their eyes as such can't see: eternal power, for instance, and the mystery of God's divine being' (Romans 1: 19–20). What does God's creation tell you about God?

9   God, the creator of this amazing world, knows and loves you in the deepest way possible. Spend some time thanking God for God's love, for God's care, for God's presence in your life. Then just rest in God's presence, enjoying God's love.

10 When you are ready, go back and join the others. But carry this still moment with you.

Prayer Cords

WHAT HAPPENS?

People make a prayer cord with knots or beads on it, to give a structure to their prayers and to remind them to pray.

EFFORT INVOLVED

MATERIALS NEEDED

- Leather cord, or waxed cotton cord
- Scissors
- Beads that will thread onto the cord
- Small bowls or cups for the beads
- Music to play during the creating of the prayer cords.

SOME THOUGHTS

Prayer is often an invisible and silent activity, with nothing to show that it has happened. It challenges our results-driven culture, where everything has to be measured, and recorded, and backed up with evidence. I need to resist the voice that tells me 'Nothing has happened' when I've been sitting quietly praying.

But I also know that the invisible and intangible nature of prayer can mean that I forget to do it, or that I give up when I can't find the right words, or that I rush through it, or my mind wanders.

How do we hold together those two realities? I have grown to appreciate tools like prayer cords that can remind me to pray, or provide a structure to my prayers, and that help me to linger in God's presence.

Prayer cords with beads or knots on them have been used for centuries by Christians, as well as people of other faiths. People feel the knots or beads as they pray, working their way along the cord.

HOW TO DO IT

You can buy beads and cord at specialist shops, or online. If you can, choose beautiful glass beads rather than mass-produced plastic ones. You need to make sure that the hole through the bead means it will easily fit onto the leather cord, but is not so big that it can't be held in place with a knot.

Make a prayer cord yourself, to show people what to do. Take a piece of cord about 50cm long and five beads. Tie a knot about 10 cm from one end of the cord. Thread a bead onto the longer end of the cord from the knot.

Tie a second knot on the other side of this bead, so that it is caught between two knots and won't move up and down the cord. If the holes in the beads are quite large, you may need to do a double knot on one or both sides to hold them in place.

For your second bead, tie a knot about 3 centimetres away from your first bead. Thread the second bead on from the long end, and secure it with another knot on its other side.

Continue attaching the beads to the cord, with a knot each side, leaving about 3 centimetres between the beads. When your cord has five beads on it, knot the two ends together and trim the ends. It should be long enough to be worn on your wrist, or it will fit easily into a pocket.

You can of course make a prayer cord of any length, with any number of beads. You can also make knots on the cord, spacing them out with your fingers, instead of using beads.

There are different ways to use the cord to pray. You could use each bead to remind you to pray for a different person. It could be people in your family, or people that you know who are ill, or friends that you want to come to know the Lord. Hold each bead in turn, praying for that person. Go round the cord as many times as you want to.

Or use this structure to pray: Thank you, Lord; Lord, have mercy; Your kingdom come. Hold each bead in turn and pray prayers of thanks, thanking God for specific things if you want to, or just offering up a general prayer of thankfulness. Then go round the cord asking God to have mercy on you, naming things that you want to confess to God. Finally go round one more time, praying for God's kingdom to come and again naming specific things before God if you want to.

Or you can use the cord to pray the Jesus prayer: Lord Jesus Christ, Son of God, have mercy on me, a sinner. Say the prayer for each knot or bead on your prayer cord.

Use your prayer cord for a week or so before doing the activity with young people, so that you can talk about it from your experience.

To do the activity with young people, cut the cord into appropriate lengths and have the beads easily accessible. Show people the prayer cord you have made and talk about the reason for making them. Suggest things that the beads could represent and ways in which people might use the cord to pray. Invite people to make their cords in an attitude of prayer and worship. You may like to play some worship music as people do this.

CONNECTING WITH SCRIPTURE

God told the Israelites to make tassels on the corners of their garments to remind them of God's commandments (Numbers 15:37–41). Jesus warned against doing this for show, or to impress others (Matthew 23:5).

HAND IT OVER

Young people can wear these prayer cords on their wrists, or carry them in their pockets, to remind them to pray. Boys may respond better if you refer to the beads as 'stones'[14] and avoid calling them prayer 'bracelets', although wristbands and surfer bracelets are very popular with some boys.

---

14 Wisdom from Brian Spurling, Urban Saints.

Easing in and out of Prayer

WHAT HAPPENS?

Suggestions for ways to lead people into contemplative prayer and silence, and then to lead them out of it.

EFFORT INVOLVED

MATERIALS NEEDED

- Large candles and matches
- Instrumental music.

SOME THOUGHTS

We need help to become silent. It can be too big a leap to leave the clamour and busyness of chatting to friends and to suddenly be quiet. The contrast can jar, and our minds and hearts can be stuck on what has been happening before, making it difficult to relax into what now is. Think about how these simple rituals can help to ease your group into and out of silence.

HOW TO DO IT

Environment

Is there a different room that you can use for times of quiet and prayer? The physical act of going into another room can help us make the transition from activity to stillness.

If that's not possible, then take time to make the space you are in feel different. Remove anything that might cause a distraction.

Have cushions on the floor that people can sit on, or space for people to lie down.

Low lights will help people to relax and to realize that they are not on show.

Ask people to take off their shoes, as a sign that they are on holy ground in God's presence. It's also asking them to take a step of vulnerability, which may help them to be more open to God.

Music

Play some instrumental music as people gather for prayer, which will cover the noise of people settling down and getting comfortable. Turn this down at the start of the prayer, so that people gradually move into silence.

Some groups will find complete silence too uncomfortable, so feel free to play gentle music throughout the time of prayer. Make sure that it doesn't have a distinct beat, or words, unless you want to provide something specific for people to focus on.

Candles

Light a candle at the start of the prayer, as a reminder of the presence of God with you. You could use a simple prayer as you light it, which one of the group could say.

Using the same candle over a period of weeks or months will mean that your group can watch it getting smaller and will have a visual reminder of the time they have spent in prayer.

A scented candle will provide another cue that enables people to prepare themselves for prayer.

Easing out of Prayer

When the prayer or time of quiet is over, tell people that it has ended. Invite people to bring their attention back to the room. Invite them to sit up or to open their eyes.

You could extinguish the candle, reminding people that they need to carry the light of Christ out with them.

If you have been playing music, now might be the time to turn it off, or to play a different type of music. If there has been silence, now might be the time to play music.

If you are in a different room, invite people to go back to your normal meeting place once they are ready. Turn the light back up.

Move through these steps gradually, rather than allowing them to happen all at once, so that people can make the journey back into conversation and interaction.

CONNECTING WITH SCRIPTURE

The Israelites sang songs as they went to Jerusalem for the three main festivals of the year. These were called 'songs of ascents' because the city was built on hills. The songs would have been a ritual that prepared their hearts and minds for worship (Psalms 121–134).

HAND IT OVER

Give young people an opportunity to lead these rituals at the beginning of prayer, which will empower them to be more connected and engaged. Ask them in what other ways the environment might help them to find stillness.

Guided Meditation

What Happens?

You lead young people through a guided meditation based on the story of Zaccheus, creating space for them to respond to God.

Effort Involved

Materials Needed

You may like to play some quiet music in the background.

Some Thoughts

Guided meditation creates a space for young people to linger with a Bible passage or an imaginary scene and to encounter God within it. It enables them to consider how that passage applies to them, and what God might be calling them to. Opportunities for prayer and discussion afterwards can make sure that their responses are not too subjective or off the wall, and can be a useful opportunity to guide people in the teachings of Jesus.

How to Do it

Use the suggestions for easing people in and out of prayer to create a conducive environment for this activity. You may want to do a stilling exercise before you read this script. Do check it through and adapt as necessary for your group. You will need to leave pauses in appropriate places, to create space for them to pray.

You live in a town called Jericho, and you've just heard that Jesus is passing through.

It's a hot day. You can feel the sun beating down on your head. You can smell the smoke from a wood fire and the meat roasting on it. You can hear the excited chatter of people talking about Jesus and how they want to see him. You can see people rushing past, some pushing others out of the way. You follow the crowd. Do you try to keep up? Do you play it cool and stroll along? Do you want to run in the opposite direction? Or are you at the front, leading the way? Talk to Jesus now, and tell him how you feel about going to meet him.

There's a big crowd lining the road, either side. Parents hold their children up so they can see over the tops of people's heads. Other children crawl through the forest of legs and sit at the front, craning their necks for a sight of Jesus. You see Zacchaeus, the wealthy tax collector, joining the crowd. He got his wealth by cheating people – no wonder everyone hates him. People are making faces at him, turning away, ignoring him. He's short, so he can't see over the heads of the people in front. He tries to push through, but no one's giving way. Then he spots a tree a little way ahead. He runs up to it and starts to climb. You watch him struggling up the tree. He's clearly desperate to see Jesus. What about you? How badly do you want to see Jesus? Tell him what's on your mind.

A shout goes up – Jesus is here! He walks along, smiling, stopping every so often to talk to people. He comes closer, and then he's stopping in front of you. You can see love and acceptance in his eyes. He's really pleased to see you. What do you say to him? Jesus listens to what you have to say. What does he say to you?

Jesus asks you to walk with him. And then he spots Zacchaeus, up the tree. You both go over. Jesus looks up at him and says, 'Zacchaeus, come down immediately. I must stay at your house today.' The three of you walk on to Zacchaeus' house, where he welcomes you in and gives you food. Other people are muttering about Jesus being friends with a sinner. But you know that, like Zacchaeus, you've done things that are wrong. In what ways have you sinned? Talk to Jesus about the things you regret.

Jesus listens to you, and you know that he forgives all the stuff you've done wrong. Just being with Jesus is an amazing experience. You feel like he knows everything about you, and he loves you deeply. You feel safe with him, as if you can just be yourself, without pretending or putting on an act.

Zacchaeus seems to feel the same. He stands up and says to Jesus that he'll give half his wealth to the poor and he'll pay back the people he's cheated. What about you? Does being with Jesus make you want to do anything differently? What might Jesus be inviting you to do with your life? Talk to Jesus about that now.

Jesus is full of joy. He says, 'This is what my life's work is all about. I came here for people like you.' It's time for him to go, but you know that somehow he'll stay with you. What do you want to take back home with you from this encounter with Jesus? Spend some time talking to Jesus about that now.

Bring people out of this meditation carefully, easing the transition back into noise and activity. You could provide space for a creative response to what people thought and experienced, or an opportunity to discuss and pray about it.

Connecting with Scripture

The story of Zacchaeus' encounter with Jesus is found in Luke 19:1–10.

Hand it Over

You could encourage young people to write their own meditations based on stories of Jesus from the Gospels. Take time to go through what they have written with them, using the opportunity to talk about the life of Jesus and what he taught. Then let them lead their peers in meditation.

Relax

What Happens?

Lead people through a deliberate relaxation of their body, as a way of still-ing themselves in order to pray.

Effort Involved

● ◉ ◉

Materials Needed

You may like to play some music in the background.

Some Thoughts

We use different words to describe ourselves – 'body' meaning our physi-cal selves; 'spirit' meaning the part of us that responds to God; 'heart' meaning our emotions and the depth of our being. But can we really divide ourselves up that neatly? I'm convinced that we are far more intercon-nected than we realize; that what we do to our bodies affects our spirits and emotions, and every other way of describing ourselves.

This activity highlights the congruency between our physical bodies and our spiritual selves. If we take the time to relax our bodies, then we will find it easier to still our hearts, minds and spirits in God's presence.

How to Do it

Read the words below and decide how to adapt them to your group. Will they cope with the word 'buttocks' being mentioned? If you think this will induce fits of giggles, leave it out. Decide what this exercise will lead into – a time of quiet? Some verses from Scripture? A meditation?

Invite young people to make themselves comfortable, with their backs supported and their feet flat on the floor. Some may like to lie down; others will want to sit on cushions against the wall; others may be most comfortable sitting in a chair. Read this slowly, allowing pauses for people to act on the words:

Take a deep breath. You are in a safe place. God is here and God loves you. We're going to take a few minutes to relax our bodies as a way of becoming still in God's presence...

Start with your toes. Scrunch them up tightly... and then release them; give them a wriggle and allow them to be still.

Then circle your ankles one by one... round to the left... and then to the right. Allow them to become loose and floppy.

Point your feet and tense your calves. Hold them tight.... then relax and let them go, allowing your lower leg to be loose and still.

Next tense your thigh muscles, and your buttocks. Feel the power in these muscles, and then choose for them to be soft and relaxed.

Pull your stomach in towards your spine... Then push it out so that it bulges... And then let it find its own position between the two, so there is no tension or strain.

Hold your hands out in front of you, your arms extended as far as they will go. Push forwards and feel your shoulder blades gently move apart. Then let your arms grow heavy and let them glide back down to your lap or to the floor.

Pull your shoulders up towards your ears... then push them down. Do that again – pull them up... and push them down... then let them settle in between.

Very gently, tilt your head forward so that your chin points towards your chest. Feel the stretch in the back of your neck. Then, just as gently, tilt your head backwards, raising your chin in the air. Return to a place of balance and equilibrium.

Clench your fists in front of you. Hold them as tight as you can... and then loosen them, slowly unfurling your fingers until your hands are open, palms to the ceiling, ready to receive from God.

You can then guide people into the next stage of the activity.

CONNECTING WITH SCRIPTURE

Psalm 131:2 describes beautifully the stillness that we seek in prayer: 'But I have calmed myself and quieted my ambitions. I am like a weaned child with its mother; like a weaned child I am content.'

HAND IT OVER

Having experienced this, young people can write their own version and take it in turns to lead the group into stillness and prayer.

CHAPTER 5

Team

A team is more than a collection of people who work at the same place. There needs to be a sense of common vision: of a commitment to each other and to working towards the same purpose. We do one another no favours if we are superficial or detached from one another, and the young people we work with will also miss out. They will pick up so much from the way their youth leaders interact, support one another and deal with moments of tension and potential conflict. However, good team relationships don't happen overnight. It pays to invest in developing a team, encouraging openness, vulnerability and honesty by modelling those qualities.

These activities provide opportunities for people within a team to grow together in relationship to God and to each other. Use them when you get together regularly with your team, or if that is not possible, then organize a retreat day every so often. Many volunteer youth workers are incredibly busy, giving up valuable time alongside jobs or caring for children. You may hesitate before expecting them to devote even more to the youth work, but encourage them to see it as an opportunity for their own growth and development, as well as contributing to what they have to offer to the young people. As you lead any of these activities, become fully involved in them. The level of engagement and vulnerability that you show will set the tone for everyone else.

Listening Exercise

WHAT HAPPENS?

Each person is given the same number of dried beans. Each time they contribute to a discussion, they 'spend' one of their beans. When they have no more beans, they have to stop talking.

EFFORT INVOLVED

● ● ●

MATERIALS NEEDED

- Dried kidney beans or chick peas: five for each member of your team.

SOME THOUGHTS

How good are your team at discussing issues? Often groups of people get into patterns of communication. Some people will always dominate a discussion; some people will always seem to have hardly anything to say. And it can be difficult to break out of those patterns, unless you try something different.

This activity may feel rather contrived, but it illustrates an important point – that everyone has a contribution to make, and if people don't make it then they have wasted their 'conversational capital'. You'll find that at the end of the conversations, people who still hold beans have more power. Some people who don't often speak up will decide to speak early, to 'spend' their beans more quickly, so they aren't left at the end trying to think of things to say. But that in itself can be an empowering experience that affects how they will contribute to future conversations.

HOW TO DO IT

Choose a topic for the conversation. It needs to be something that people care about, so that they have lots to say. It could be work-related: what topics should you study with your youth group next term? What's the best way to deal with bad behaviour? Or it may be about church, or simply life in general.

Give everyone five dried beans. Tell them that in the conversation that you are about to have, every time they talk, they will 'spend' one of the beans by placing it in the centre of the group. When they run out of beans, they aren't allowed to say anything else. Introduce the topic, with any explanation (this counts as one of your beans!), and allow the conversation to develop. If everyone spends all their beans and there is clearly more to say on the topic, then allocate another three or four to each person.

Get people to reflect on this experience. How did the restriction of the beans affect the way they contributed to the conversation? What was it like to run out of beans when you still had more to say? What was it like to have beans when most other people had run out? Did you say more or less than you might say in a discussion without beans?

Then get people discussing the way in which team discussions normally take place! Are there things they would like to change?

CONNECTING WITH SCRIPTURE
- James said that everyone should be quick to listen, slow to speak and slow to become angry (James 1:19).
- Paul says that we are the body of Christ, all with a part to play. If any of us opt out or are excluded, then the whole body suffers (1 Corinthians 12:12–31).

To-Do Lists

WHAT HAPPENS?

Before entering the room where you will meet, people take time to write their 'to-do' lists on postcards and pin them to a washing line.

EFFORT INVOLVED

● ○ ○

MATERIALS NEEDED

- Washing line and pegs
- Postcards and pens.

SOME THOUGHTS

There is nothing more frustrating than being in a meeting where people aren't fully engaged, because they have things on their mind, or are texting on their phones, or have their laptops open looking things up on the internet! Wherever you are, be there. We give people a precious gift by being fully present to them.

Having said that, it can be difficult to focus on the moment if your head is full of all the other things you have to do once the day gets under way. This exercise helps people to offload their to-do lists and to come back to them later. It also signals to them that you expect them to be focused on what you are doing together.

HOW TO DO IT

Hang up a washing line outside your meeting room. Have a pile of postcards and pens there. Meet people outside the room and invite them to sit down with a postcard and pen. Explain the activity – that in a moment you want them to write down all the things on their minds: things they have to do; worries and responsibilities; things they don't want to forget.

Then invite people to become still: to take a deep breath. Lead people in prayer, thanking God for God's presence with you, and asking God to bring to mind all the things that we need to lay aside to focus on the business we need to do. Then invite people to write all those things on the postcard. When they are ready, they can peg them on the washing line and then join you in the room where you will meet.

Once your meeting is over, people can collect their postcards and take them away with them.

CONNECTING WITH SCRIPTURE

Jesus managed to be fully present to people around him. On the way to heal Jairus' daughter, with crowds pressing around him, he knew that someone had touched him with the intention of being healed. And he turned his attention on her, to affirm her action (Luke 8:40–48).

Lectio Divina

WHAT HAPPENS?

You read a passage of Scripture slowly a number of times, giving space and structure for people to reflect on it.

EFFORT INVOLVED

● ● ●

MATERIALS NEEDED

A Bible.

SOME THOUGHTS

Lectio Divina is Latin for 'holy reading', and it comes out of the Benedictine tradition. It's a slow and prayerful way of lingering with a text from the Bible, chewing it over and letting it lead us into contemplation. This way of reading is not about getting information, or being educated, or being entertained, or escaping. It's about encountering God through God's word. Scripture becomes a meeting place where we spend some time with the one who loves us.

Lectio Divina can sound complicated when it's described, but in fact it's very simple. There are four stages to it.

Reading – Lectio

Read a short passage from the Bible slowly, allowing the word of God to settle into your heart and mind.

Meditation – Meditatio

Read the passage again a number of times, listening for a word or phrase that stands out. Repeat this to yourself, chewing it over and listening to the thoughts, feelings and images that arise from it. Linger with the passage – don't rush.

Prayer – Oratio

Let your meditation lead you into prayer. Talk to God about what you have been thinking and feeling, secure in the knowledge that God knows and loves you.

Contemplation – Contemplatio

When you have run out of words, be still in God's presence, trusting that God will lead you where you need to go in response to this passage.

In fact, you may go through those stages in a different order. You may find you start with praying about lots of concerns; you may find you go from reading to prayer to reading to silence to reading to prayer again. It doesn't matter. 'Pray as you can, not as you can't.' Come to God's word with the intention of meeting God.

How to Do it

Use this structure to lead people in Lectio Divina, making the words your own. You'll need to choose a Bible passage to read. It could be one that you are going to study with the youth group over the coming weeks.

Acknowledge with the group that some people find it easier to sit still than others. Some people may like to stand up and move around as they listen; others may want to write things down. Encourage people to find a space and posture where they are comfortable.

Invite people to become still in God's presence. You could use the breathing prayer or stilling meditation from the 'Contemplation' section of this book.

Tell people what passage you are going to read. Invite them to simply listen to the words, the first time through.

Read the passage for the first time and leave a short period of silence afterwards.

Then tell people that you are going to read the passage a second time, and they should listen out for a word or phrase that stands out for them. After you finish reading, you'll leave a short period of silence in which they should repeat that word or phrase to themselves, over and over, drawing out its flavour and complexity.

Read the passage for the second time and leave a short period of silence afterwards.

Tell people that you are going to read the same passage a third time. This time, they should think about how it touches their life at the moment. In the silence after the reading they should linger with that thought, repeating any words or phrases from the passage that resonate with them.

Read the passage for the third time and leave a short period of silence afterwards.

Tell people that you are going to read the passage for the final time. This time, as they listen to it they should think about what God is calling them to do or be in response to this passage, and meditate on that in the silence afterwards.

Read the passage for the final time and leave a short period of silence afterwards.

Then invite people to bring their thoughts and feelings to God in prayer, and when they have run out of words simply to rest in God's presence, in silence and peace, confident that God loves and accepts them.

Leave a longer period of silence.

When you sense that people have prayed for long enough, invite people to return their attention to the room. You may like to lead a prayer, thanking God for God's word and what people have heard from it.

As you feel it to be appropriate, invite people to share what they have received from God during that time.

Connecting with Scripture

- The Bible is not just a book. The writer to the Hebrews tells us that the word of God is alive and active (Hebrews 4:12).
- The psalmist says he has hidden God's word in his heart and clearly makes God's word a priority (Psalm 119:9–16).

Landscape

WHAT HAPPENS?

People use a landscape to identify where in their lives they are experiencing refreshment and dryness, and what are their highs and lows.

EFFORT INVOLVED

MATERIALS NEEDED

- A large sheet of paper and a marker pen, or cloth and some gravel
- Rocks, a shallow bowl of water, sand and a piece of dark cloth
- A pipe cleaner for each person
- Music to play in the background.

SOME THOUGHTS

It's easy in team meetings to rush into business without finding out how people are. And yet the internal state of your team will affect what they contribute to the session and what you all get out of it. This activity will allow you to go deeper than 'How are you?' – 'I'm fine', by giving people a creative context in which to answer the question.

HOW TO DO IT

On the large sheet of paper, draw a wide road, snaking along from one end to the other. Or use gravel to mark out the edges of a road on the piece of cloth. By the side of the road, use the other materials to mark out the landscape: the rocks represent mountains; the bowl of water, a lake; the sand, a desert; and the dark cloth, a valley.

Give each person a pipe cleaner and ask them to make a figure or symbol that represents themselves. Introduce the landscape by saying something like this:

Imagine that this road represents the journey of your life recently. The rocks are the mountain-top experiences, where everything has gone brilliantly and you've sensed God with you; the water is a lake where you have felt refreshed and energized; the sand is a desert where you have felt dry and far from God; the dark cloth is a valley where you have felt low and afraid.

Take some time to think about which of those four aspects have featured in your life recently – maybe some, maybe all. What has caused them? Which has been strongest?

Play some music and allow people to reflect on the landscape. After an appropriate period of time, lead the way in talking about how you relate to those four elements of the landscape. Move your figure along the road, explaining where you have experienced highs and lows, refreshment and dryness. The level of openness and honesty that you use will set the tone for the activity and will encourage people to respond in a similar way. Leave your figure by the aspect of the landscape that is strongest in your life at the moment.

Invite other people to talk about their own experiences in a similar way. When everyone has contributed, get people to pray for one another, in small groups or all together.

Connecting with Scripture

Proverbs 18:24 says: 'One who has unreliable friends soon comes to ruin, but there is a friend who sticks closer than a brother.' Encourage your team to be that kind of friend to one another, by being honest about where they're at and supporting one another in it.

Twenty Questions

WHAT HAPPENS?

Two people are given an envelope with 20 questions inside. They take it in turns to pull out a question and answer it.[15]

EFFORT INVOLVED

● ○ ○

MATERIALS NEEDED

- Copies of the questions sheet
- Envelopes
- Scissors.

SOME THOUGHTS

How well do you know the other people in your team? This activity gives you the opportunity to find out new and probably surprising things. It gives people an invitation to talk about some things that don't normally come up in conversation, as well as finding out some trivia about each other. You could pick up on some of these themes and explore them further with your team.

HOW TO DO IT

You need one envelope and one sheet of questions for each pair of people in your team. Cut each sheet into strips, fold them and put them in an envelope.

Get people into pairs – you can decide whether you'll encourage people to join someone they don't know very well. Give each pair an envelope. One person draws out a question and asks it of their partner, who answers as honestly as they feel comfortably able. Conversations may develop from the questions, and the person who answers should feel free to ask the same thing of their questioner.

Allow about 20 minutes for this. Invite people to reflect on what they learned about each other.

---

15 I first came across this idea many years ago in one of Pip Wilson's books. More recently, Bruce Stanley has posted something similar on his site: www.embody.co.uk.

CONNECTING WITH SCRIPTURE

Jesus seemed to ask people a lot of questions: 'What do you think about the Messiah?' to the Pharisees in Matthew 22:42; 'Why do you call me good?' to the ruler in Luke 18:19.

Who was your favourite Blue Peter presenter?

What song would you sing at a karaoke evening?

When did you last cry, and why?

Who cleans your toilet?

If your best friend's wedding clashed with your mum's birthday party, which would you go to, and why?

What would you change about your church, if you could?

If you had a one-to-one meeting with the Prime Minister, what would you talk about?

Who is the most inspiring woman that you know?

Have you ever shoplifted? Tell the story.

Porridge, toast, or cereal for breakfast?

What would you do if you weren't afraid?

What do you hope you are doing in ten years' time?

What were you afraid of when you were five, and when did you stop fearing it?

What does your inner critic say to you most often, and how do you respond?

Imagine you could have a month's sabbatical anywhere in the world. Where would you go?

When did you last do something that you had never done before?

What colour is the inside of your head?

Who are you looking forward to meeting in heaven?

Which reality TV show would you most like to go on, or least like to, and why?

What question were you most dreading?

Object Metaphors

What Happens?

Team members bring items that represent how they feel about the youth work, and how they would like it to be.[16]

Effort Involved

Materials Needed

People will need to find their own materials before you meet.

Some Thoughts

This is a great way to get people to contribute to strategy and vision for your group. It reveals different and often surprising facets of people's thoughts and feelings about the work you're doing at the moment and what you could be doing in the future.

To give you some examples, this is what people brought when we did this at Grace.

Items that represented something we're doing well:

- A dial-up cable – the connectivity between us and God and between people
- Vampire blood – something different and unexpected!
- Stained-glass window – the skills and gifts that people bring.

Items that represented things we felt were missing:

- Newspaper – it can feel like a special event that happens every so often; needs to connect more with everyday life
- Tube map with Ealing removed and global locations added – need to have more of a local impact
- Broken plate – need to be prepared to let some things go, or die, for new to emerge.

---

16 Adam Baxter

How to Do it

You will need to give people at least a week's notice of this activity, so that they have time to think and to find a couple of objects. Don't explain in too great detail what people need to bring; allow them to use their imaginations. You might want to say something like this, either verbally or by email:

> Spend some time thinking and praying about the youth work that we do and the ways in which it might develop. Bring to our next meeting a couple of objects. One object should represent what you think we're doing well at the moment in our youth work. The other should represent something that you feel is missing from the youth work. Be creative! There are no right or wrong answers. From everyone's contributions we will build up a great picture of what we are and what we could be.

If this type of activity is new, people may feel a bit apprehensive. Assure them that whatever they bring will be valid.

Start with the objects that represent things you're doing well. Get people to explain what they have brought and why, one by one. People can ask questions of clarification to encourage others to expand on what they have brought and why, but don't allow discussion of the objects there and then; just allow the explanations to stand. When everyone has contributed, look for common themes that have been brought up by the objects and discuss these further.

Then do the same with the objects that represent things you feel are missing. Again, allow a few questions for clarification, but no discussion until all the objects are named. Again, look for common themes that have emerged, or contrasting opinions, and discuss the objects further.

Get someone to record what was brought and why, so that you can do some more work on all the ideas that have been brought. Your view of leadership will dictate how much you feel it is your role to incorporate these contributions in future vision and strategy and how much it is a shared responsibility.

Connecting with Scripture

- The prophets used symbols and acted out scenes to explain what God was going to do. Pity poor Ezekiel, who had to lie on his side for 430 days in front of a clay model of Jerusalem, and then bake his bread over cow dung! But the creative communication hit home (Ezekiel 4:1–17).

- Jesus' 'I am...' statements in John were powerful metaphors that com-
municated important aspects of his character and mission. I am the
bread of life (John 6:35–51); I am the light of the world (John 8:12 and
9:5); I am the good shepherd (John 10:11); I am the resurrection and
the life (John 11:25); I am the way, the truth and the life (John 14:6); I
am the true vine (John 15:1).

Life Journey

WHAT HAPPENS?

Team members represent pictorially the journey they have been on in life, as a way of talking about themselves.

EFFORT INVOLVED

MATERIALS NEEDED

Paper and pens.

SOME THOUGHTS

This exercise helps you get to know people in your team better by understanding where they have come from. It's something you can do as a joint exercise, where everyone works on their diagrams together and then takes it in turn to talk about them. Or you could get one person at each meeting to draw it at home and then talk about their diagram at the start. You could then take time to pray for that person.

HOW TO DO IT

Invite people to represent on a diagram the journey they have taken through life, using their creativity to communicate key events and people. They can draw turnings they have taken; dead ends; obstacles; places of rest. They could think about what type of vehicle they were travelling on during different parts of the journey. They can depict struggles, joys, opportunities and challenges. They can show the companions they have had on the journey, and where they have felt alone. They can represent the presence of God in their lives, and moments of connection or distance.

To give people an idea of how they might do this, you could draw a diagram of Joseph's life journey from Genesis 37–50. It's a real rollercoaster of ups and downs! Stress that this is just an example. Encourage people to use their imaginations to represent the uniqueness of their own journey.

Be prepared to lead the way by drawing and explaining your own diagram; the level of honesty and openness you use will set the tone for the rest of the group.

CONNECTING WITH SCRIPTURE

- Joseph had an interesting journey through life – of ups and downs, from favoured son to slave, from prison to palaces, from hated by his brothers to needed by them (Genesis 37–50).
- Timothy had the benefit of a godly mother and grandmother, who set an example for him. Who has played that role in our lives? Can we do the same for others? (2 Timothy 1:5)
- In 2 Corinthians 11:16–33, Paul catalogues the sufferings he has been through. What enables someone to rise above these challenges, rather than being defeated by them?

Fellowship

WHAT HAPPENS?

People reflect on 1 John 1 and their relationships with other people, particularly within the team. How much do they share a common life with others?

EFFORT INVOLVED

MATERIALS NEEDED

- Copies of the handout
- Pens
- You may like to play some instrumental music during the time for reflection.

SOME THOUGHTS

There's something in me that squirms when I hear the word 'fellowship'. It conjures up images of standing around after church services with a cup of bad coffee trying to make polite conversation, in the hope that you'll somehow attain this thing called 'fellowship', or of feeling obliged to endure dried-out sandwiches and nasty cakes at a 'fellowship tea' in a dusty church hall. Mmm, what does that say about me?!

But then I read 1 John 1, where John talks about fellowship a lot: fellowship with God the Father; fellowship with Jesus, God's son; fellowship with one another; and the way these are interconnected. Fellowship means 'to share a common life'. It's not artificial small talk, or a club that you join; it's living, breathing, laughing, crying, struggling, celebrating – and all shades of experience in between – in common with other people. It's lives intertwined; it's hopes and dreams and disappointments shared; it's being real and unafraid. That's the kind of fellowship that I crave.

HOW TO DO IT

Talk about the word 'fellowship' from 1 John 1 and what it means. Invite people to discuss their experiences of fellowship, both good and bad.

Give each person a copy of the handout and a pen. Explain that they will have an opportunity to reflect on their relationship with God and with others and how far they share common life. Point out that the large circle with the small one overlapping represents their relationship with God; the smaller circle, their relationships with others. There are questions on the sheet to guide them, and the text from 1 John 1. Tell people how long they have to reflect on the sheet and explain that only each individual will see that individual's sheet.

Draw people back together. You don't necessarily want them to feed back directly from what they have drawn and written on their sheet, but to use the time of reflection to think about relationships within your team. Some questions you could discuss:

- How much of a common life do you share with others in the team? How well do you know each other? How much time do you spend with each other outside of a work context?
- How appropriate is it to 'share a common life' with others from your work? What are the dangers of being too close, and of people knowing too much about you? What are the benefits of a shared common life at work?
- Should we have different expectations of team relationships when we work with Christians?
- How do relationships in the team need to change? What can we do to develop healthy interdependent relationships and a rich, shared common life?

Connecting with Scripture

- Jesus says that the way others will know that we are his disciples is through how much we love each other (John 13:34–35).
- Ruth decided that she would share a common life with Naomi, with her heartfelt declaration that: 'Where you go I will go, and where you stay I will stay. Your people will be my people and your God my God. Where you die I will die, and there I will be buried. May the Lord deal with me, be it ever so severely, if even death separates you and me' (Ruth 1:16–17).

To share a common life...

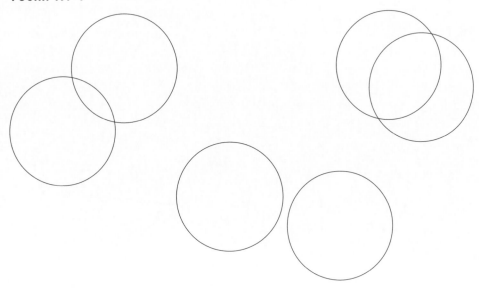

Do you try to hide anything in your relationship
with God?
How does your relationship with God
affect your relationships with others?

That which was from the beginning,
which we have heard,
which we have seen with our eyes,
which we have looked at and our hands have touched –
this we proclaim concerning the Word of life.
The life appeared; we have seen it and testify to it, and we proclaim to you the
eternal life, which was with the Father and has appeared to us. We proclaim
to you what we have seen and heard, so that you also may have fellowship
with us. And our fellowship is with the Father and with his Son, Jesus Christ.
We write this to make our joy complete.
This is the message we have heard from him and declare to you: God is light;
in him there is no darkness at all. If we claim to have fellowship with him and
yet walk in the darkness, we lie and do not live out the truth. But if we walk
in the light, as he is in the light, we have fellowship with one another, and the
blood of Jesus, his Son, purifies us from all sin.
1 John 1:1–7

How much of a common life do you share with others? Add names to the circles above, to represent relationships in your life. The overlap shows how much of a common life you share.

What do you withhold from others that you need to share?

Is the overlap too big in any relationship? Are you too possessive or dependent?

How can you create a common life where there isn't one at the moment?

Which friendships are you most grateful for?

Colour Supplements

What Happens?

People are given a colour supplement each and a topic to brainstorm. They look for images and phrases connected with or inspired by the topic.

Effort Involved

Materials Needed

Colour supplements – the magazines that come with newspapers at the weekend. You'll need one per person.

Some Thoughts

A brainstorm is a way of generating lots of ideas, from which you can choose ones that will work for your context. Often, however, they can run out of steam before they have even got started. Some people don't respond well to the pressure to be creative; they end up like the proverbial rabbit in the headlights, with a completely blank mind. Others start to judge and evaluate ideas, even though they know they shouldn't, effectively pouring cold water on any further contributions.

This activity facilitates the generation of plenty of ideas, by adding some constraints and by providing a pool from which to fish for ideas. Giving people time to think on their own gives everyone an opportunity to contribute, not merely the most vocal.

The following example uses a Guardian weekend magazine and the topic 'the Holy Spirit'. Remember that this would be presented much more visually during the activity, with images and words torn from the magazine.

- The word 'inspiration', from an ice-cream advert
- The phrase 'energy source', from an advert about the Algarve
- A picture of glasses – is the Spirit the 'lenses' through which we see God?
- Children playing with foam and bubbles – the Spirit cleanses and renews us
- Pictures of Burma after the cyclone – the wind of the Spirit – how violent is it? Does it cause damage?

- The phrase 'Let's play' – is there something playful about God's Spirit?
- Photographs of the best open-water swimming spots in Britain – particularly one where a wave is crashing over the edge of the pool. The exhilaration, freedom and refreshment of being immersed in God's Spirit.
- A picture of someone on a trampoline – able to jump higher – the Spirit anoints our gifts and enables us to go further
- An article on al fresco living, with pictures of furniture outdoors, entitled 'Walls optional' – how do we try to box in the Spirit? What walls do we put up?

Remember: these are the ideas without evaluation. Some may be more helpful than others. Some may need to be discarded; but that can be a useful exercise in itself, working out why your initial ideas don't really work.

How to Do it

Hand out copies of the supplements and explain the idea. The participants are to look through them and tear out words, phrases and images that connect with the topic of your brainstorm. They should allow their imaginations free rein, and should not judge their ideas. Tell them how much time they have got.

Then get people to share their ideas one by one. Stress that everyone's ideas are equally valuable. It doesn't matter if they repeat what someone else has said. And no one is allowed to say, 'I'm not very creative,' or to put down their contribution.

Once everyone's ideas are out in the open, start to pool together similar ideas. Are any common themes evolving? Do any ideas stand out? Do any need clarification? Do any include aspects that aren't helpful? You can then decide which ideas you'll take forward for the particular context that you are working on.

Connecting with Scripture

Jesus used examples from everyday life in his parables: a farmer sowing seed (Matthew 13:3); a woman kneading yeast into dough (Matthew 13:33); and a woman looking for a lost coin (Luke 15:8).

Eating Together

WHAT HAPPENS?

Have a team meal together: an intentional time of building community and sharing lives.

EFFORT INVOLVED

MATERIALS NEEDED

- Great food: see suggestions below
- Some of the following, depending on what activities you do:
  - A large bowl of warm water, soap and towel
  - Three candles and matches
  - Nightlights
  - Bread and wine.

SOME THOUGHTS

Amazing things happen around meal tables. Friendships are strengthened; people are affirmed; problems are dissected; and the world is put to rights. Having people round for a meal is about more than feeding people's bodies; you are creating a space where whole selves can be nurtured and sustained. So this may be a very obvious suggestion, but it's an important one and a great opportunity to do what Jesus did.

HOW TO DO IT

Some suggestions are made here for how to be intentional about building a community during the meal. You won't want to use all of them, but pick some that fit the people who'll be there.

Have food to share

Serve food on big platters, so that everyone can help themselves from a central place. Dips with chopped vegetables or warmed pitta make a great starter, as do antipasti from the deli, which don't involve any cooking. Remember to check whether any of the group are vegetarians or vegans or have food allergies. If people offer to bring something, say 'Yes please.' Don't feel you have to be a hero and cook everything, even if that is well within your capabilities. Allowing people to contribute food or help with preparation or washing-up gives them an opportunity to give and helps them feel more relaxed, needed and involved.

Washing Hands
Ask someone to help by holding a large bowl of warm water or a towel. Then go round and wash everyone's hands before the meal, as a sign of welcome. Touch helps to break down barriers and is very affirming; but allow people to opt out, if it makes them feel uncomfortable, without making a big deal out of it.

Lighting Candles
Ask someone to light three candles in the centre of the table as you sit down to eat, to remind you of the presence of the Father, Son and Spirit. Pray before you eat together.

Find Out How People Are
Choose one or two of the questions from the 'Twenty Questions' activity (page 174), to go beyond 'How are you?' and discover what is happening in people's lives. Or invite people to bring a photograph with them showing a time in their lives that they like to remember and get people to talk about these while you eat.

Toast One Another
Invite people to propose toasts at any point during the meal, affirming what members of the team have done recently. Watch to make sure that everyone that needs to be is included.

Tell a Story
Tell the story of the wedding banquet from Luke 14:15–24 and get people to discuss it in the context of the youth work that you do. If your youth work was a meal, what kind would it be: a wedding banquet, a 'bargain bucket' from a fast-food restaurant, a school dinner...? What excuses do people give when you invite them to things? What is really going on behind those excuses? Who, for you, are 'the poor, the crippled, the blind, the lame'? How good are you at including them?

Invite Stories
Invite people to tell stories – about when they experienced love, or the time they did something they were afraid of, or the day they left home, or the last time they cried – or something less challenging, such as the

best sports event they ever attended, or the achievement they are most proud of.

Pray for One Another

Invite people to share things that they would like prayer for. Have a pile of unlit nightlights on the table. Invite people to light one as they pray for each person and to put it among the dishes on the table.

Share Bread and Wine

End the meal by sharing bread and wine together informally around the table. Use the opportunity to speak words of blessing over one another as you pass round the bread and wine.

CONNECTING WITH SCRIPTURE

- Jesus had dinner at the house of a Pharisee (Luke 7:36–50), and with a crowd of tax collectors and sinners (Matthew 9:10); he hosted the Passover supper for his disciples as the cross beckoned (Matthew 26:17–30), and then cooked breakfast on a beach for them after he had defeated death (John 21:12–14).
- Jesus told stories about feasts – about picking the place of honour at a banquet (Luke 14:7–14), and about the wedding banquet where the guests refused to come, so people were invited in off the streets (Matthew 22:1–14).

Youthwork the partnership
- The Initiatives

YOUTHWORK THE PARTNERSHIP

 ALOVE (The Salvation Army for a new generation), Oasis, schoolswork.co.uk, Spring Harvest, Youth for Christ and Youthwork magazine are working together to equip and resource the church for effective youthwork and ministry.

The partnership exists to offer support, encouragement and ideas for busy youth workers including:

YOUTHWORK THE CONFERENCE

 Youthwork the conference is a weekend event designed for church-based volunteer youth workers, with specific streams for younger leaders and salaried youth workers. *Youthwork the conference* has been designed to give training and support by offering encouragement, ideas and resources to busy youth workers. There is also an additional 24 hour Retreat Day.

The conference includes: Main plenary sessions with teaching, worship, prayer, reflection and encouragement plus many practical and skills based seminars covering a wide range of youthwork issues. There are also opportunities to network with others; space to reflect and pray, and access to a large range of youth ministry specialist agencies via an extensive exhibition and resource area.

Youthwork the conference takes place each November. Visit www.youthwork.co.uk/conference or call 01825 746535 for more information.

Youthwork the conference is administrated by Spring Harvest.

YOUTHWORK MAGAZINE

 Since 1992, *Youthwork magazine* has been the magazine of choice for youth workers across the UK. Every issue is packed with resources, information and opinion, providing youth workers with all the latest news on youth ministry and youth culture. Each month there are book, cd and resource reviews, challenging and inspiring articles, Jobsearch, must-see websites, and a pull-out section packed with ready-to-use curriculum resources including drama, discussion triggers, and ways to use music and film with your group. With all this and more jammed into every issue, it's no surprise that so many youth workers consider *Youthwork magazine* essential reading.

On sale in most Christian bookshops. Visit www.youthwork.co.uk/magazine or call 01892 652364 for more information or to subscribe.

Youthwork magazine is published by CCP Limited.

YOUTHWORK THE RESOURCES

 Youthwork the resources is a series of original books to help youth workers in their youthwork and ministry. From quick-fire creative ideas to challenging thinking on the theory and theology of youthwork, this series is designed with one aim in mind - resourcing YOU, the youth worker.

Series editors: Damian Wharton & Martin Saunders

Visit www.youthwork.co.uk/resources for more information.

Youthwork magazine are published by Monarch.

YOUTHWORK THE TRAINING

What Every Volunteer Youth Worker Should Know

 A training course for busy 'extra timers' who need to know the basics – and fast! This innovative course provides a foundation of knowledge, tips and resources in an accessible and practical format. The course is made up of 9 two-hour sessions which may be delivered in a variety of ways to fit needs and lifestyle! You can choose when and where you do the sessions.

Participation includes a free resource book and 100 ready-to-use ideas. The course is endorsed by a broad spectrum of Christian denominations and networks.

Visit www.youthwork.co.uk/training/volunteerscourse or call 0207 450 9044 for more information.

'What Every Volunteer Youthworker Should Know' is managed and delivered by Oasis.

The Art of Connecting

A resource to equip you and your youth group to see lives changed... forever! The vision behind 'The Art of Connecting' is the realisation that people communicate most naturally when they are exploring their own stories together. The course aims to empower people to share their faith through story - making connections between their story, their friends' stories and God's story.

'The Art of Connecting' book and Leaders Pack are available, as are regional training days for youth leaders and young people.

Visit www.youthwork.co.uk/training/aoc or call 0121 550 8055 for more information.

'The Art of Connecting' is developed and delivered by Youth for Christ.

YOUTHWORK ONLINE

 www.youthwork.co.uk features a dynamic home page updated weekly with the latest information, news analysis and views on youthwork and youth culture - all things that will be of interest to all those working with young people. It's also the place to find out about the partnership and how we can support you, including more details on the conference, magazine, training courses, and resources, and access to the Youthwork online directory.

At www.youthwork.co.uk/community there is a range of online discussion forums with discussions on youth ministry issues, plus forums to share and resources with other youth workers from across the country.

Visit www.youthwork.co.uk for more information.

Youthwork online is owned by CCP Limited and developed by all the partners.

YOUTHWORK THE PARTNERSHIP - THE PARTNERS

ALOVE
The Salvation Army for a new generation

 ALOVE is The Salvation Army for a new generation. ALOVE is calling a generation to dynamic faith, radical lifestyle, adventurous mission and a fight for justice.

ALOVE provides young people and young adults with ongoing opportunities to engage in culturally engaging worship, cell and small group discipleship, innovative mission and world changing social action.

ALOVE runs training programmes to develop leaders and missionaries for the 21st century. ALOVE is also pioneering new expressions of church, youth work and social inclusion in communities around the United Kingdom and Ireland.

To find out more about ALOVE:

Visit: www.salvationarmy.org.uk/ALOVE
Email: ALOVE@salvationarmy.org.uk
Phone: 0208 288 1202

Write to: ALOVE UK, The Salvation Army, 21 Crown Lane, Morden, Surrey, SM4 5BY, England.

Oasis

 Oasis develops effective ways of transforming the lives of the poor and marginalised and whole communities in the UK and around the world. We help churches and individuals do the same.

Drawing on 20 years experience of pioneering mission, education and youth work initiatives; Oasis provides opportunities for young people to participate in life changing UK and Global mission on both a short and long term basis and equips youth workers with innovative resources and training including the 'What Every Volunteer Youth Worker Should Know' course & the JNC-qualifying Oasis Youth Work and Ministry Degree.

Oasis also enables youth workers and church volunteers to support young people's personal, social and health education in their local schools through training associate educators in Sex and Relationships Education and Mentoring as well as tackling social exclusion among young people head on through the delivery of one to one transition work, mentoring and supported housing programmes.

To find out more about Oasis:

Visit: www.oasistrust.org
Email: enquiries@oasistrust.org
Phone: 0207 450 9000
Write to: Oasis, The Oasis Centre, 115 Southwark Bridge Road, London, SE1 0AX, England.

Schoolswork.co.uk

 schoolswork.co.uk is a collaboration of schools and youth workers across the UK who regularly step in to the world of education to offer their services and support. We offer a mix of inspiration, resources and training for this crucial area of youthwork.

With the role of faith and spirituality in education changing, schoolswork. co.uk is passionate about facilitating a new and dynamic response to these challenges, developing and deepening the skills of Christians visiting schools, and fostering a new vision for the church's contribution to education.

To find out more about schoolswork.co.uk:

Visit: www.schoolswork.co.uk
Email: info@schoolswork.co.uk

Phone: 01582 877330

Write to: schoolswork.co.uk, 31 Upper George Street, Luton, LU1 2QX

Spring Harvest [inc Spring Harvest logo]

 Spring Harvest's vision is to 'equip the Church for action'. Through a range of events, conferences, courses and resources we enable Christians to impact their local communities and the wider world.

Spring Harvest is probably best known for Main Event, held every Easter, which attracts over 55,000 people of all ages. Over 10,000 of those attending are young people. The Main Event also includes specific streams which cater for over 2,000 students. Alongside the teaching programme, Spring Harvest provide a range of resources for young people and those involved in youth ministry.

Through our sister company - Spring Harvest Holidays - we offer quality holidays at our four-star holiday park in the Vendée, France. These inspirational holidays cater for people of all ages in a safe, secure and relaxed environment.

The Spring Harvest range of resources - albums, books and teaching resources - all aim to equip the Church for action.

To find out more about Spring Harvest:

Visit: www.springharvest.org

Email: info@springharvest.org

Phone: 01825 769000

Write to: Spring Harvest, 14 Horsted Square, Uckfield, East Sussex, TN22 1QG, England.

Youth for Christ

 Youth for Christ (YFC), one of the most dynamic Christian organisations, are taking good news relevantly to every young person in Britain. They help tackle the big issues facing young people today. They're going out on the streets, into schools and communities and have changed the lives of countless people throughout the UK.

Their staff, trainees and volunteers currently reach over 50,000 young people each week and have over 50 centres in locations throughout the UK. They also provide creative arts and sports mission teams, a network of registered groups and a strong emphasis on 'three-story' evangelism. YFC International works in 120 nations.

To find out more about YFC:

Visit: www.yfc.co.uk
Email: churchresource@yfc.co.uk
Phone: 0121 550 8055
Write to: YFC, PO Box 5254, Halesowen, West Midlands B63 3DG, England.

Youthwork magazine

 Youthwork magazine is Britain's most widely read magazine resource for Christian youth workers. Through articles, ready-to-use resources, reviews, youthwork and cultural news and analysis, and much more, Youthwork magazine provides ideas, resources and guidance to help you in your work with young people.

Youthwork magazine is published monthly by CCP Limited, which is part of the Premier Media Group, who also publish Christianity and Christian Marketplace.

To find out more about Youthwork magazine:

Visit: www.youthwork.co.uk
Email: youthwork@premier.org.uk
Phone: 01892 652364
Write to: Youthwork Magazine, CCP Limited, Broadway House, The Broadway, Crowborough, TN6 1HQ, England.